Draw the Circle

Resources by Mark Batterson

Be a Circle Maker

The Circle Maker

The Circle Maker Video Curriculum

The Circle Maker Prayer Journal

The Circle Maker, Student Edition

Draw the Circle

In a Pit with a Lion on a Snowy Day

Praying Circles around Your Children

Primal

Soul Print

Wild Goose Chase

Draw the Circle

Circle

The 40 Day Prayer Challenge

Mark Batterson

New York Times Bestselling Author of *The Circle Maker*

ZONDERVAN.com/
AUTHORTRACKER
follow your favorite authors

ZONDERVAN

Draw the Circle
Copyright © 2012 by Mark Batterson

This title is also available as a Zondervan ebook. Visit www.zondervan.com/ebooks.

This title is also available in a Zondervan audio edition. Visit www.zondervan.fm.

Requests for information should be addressed to:

Zondervan, *Grand Rapids, Michigan 49530*

Library of Congress Cataloging-in-Publication Data

Batterson, Mark.
    Draw the circle : the 40-day prayer challenge / Mark Batterson.
        p.   cm.
    ISBN 978-0-310-32712-7 (softcover)
    1. Prayer—Christianity. I. Title.
    BV210.3.   B3785 2013
    242'.2—dc23   2012034385

Published in association with the literary agency of Fedd & Company, Inc., Post Office Box 341973, Austin, TX 78734.

Interior illustration: iStockPhoto®
Interior design: Beth Shagene

Printed in the United States of America

---

14 15 16 17 18 /DCI/ 21 20 19 18 17 16 15 14

Contents

Introduction

The forty-day prayer challenge is going to change your life. In fact, the next forty days have the potential to dramatically alter the *rest* of your life. God is going to begin a good work in you, and He is going to carry it to completion. Miracles that happen in your life decades from now will trace their origin back to this season of prayer. Breakthroughs that happen during these forty days will become generational blessings that live on long after you die.

If you press into God's presence like never before, you will experience God like never before. You'll look back on these forty days as the best forty days of your life. They won't be the easiest forty days; in fact, they may be the hardest. Don't be surprised if you experience spiritual opposition along the way. But if you pray through, God will break through in new ways. It's as inevitable as the tide coming in.

There is nothing magical about forty days, but there is something biblical about it. That's the number of days Jesus spent in the wilderness fasting and praying. It marked a critical chapter in His life — the transition from His earthly father's business to His heavenly Father's business. Jesus was tested like never before, but this experience set the stage for His greatest victories over the enemy. The war against sin and Satan may have been won on Calvary's cross, but a key battle happened in the wilderness three years earlier. When Jesus returned to Galilee, He wasn't the same person. You won't be either. You'll emerge from this forty-day prayer challenge, just like Jesus, in the power of the Holy Spirit.

If you want God to do something new in you, you cannot keep doing the same old thing. You have to do something different. And if you do, God will create new capacities within you. There will be new gifts and new revelations. But you've got to pray the price. You'll get out of this what you put into it.

How to Start a Revival

Draw the Circle is a sequel of sorts. Since the release of *The Circle Maker*, I've heard hundreds of prayer testimonies that have set my faith on fire. Almost every day I hear a new story that makes me want to applaud God. This book is my way of stewarding those testimonies by sharing them. I've also learned more about prayer since *The Circle Maker* was released than the knowledge I had beforehand. I'll share those new discoveries in the pages that follow.

So let me pick up where *The Circle Maker* left off.

Rodney "Gypsy" Smith was born on the outskirts of London in 1860. He never received a formal education, yet he lectured at Harvard. Despite his humble origins, he was invited by two sitting United States presidents to the White

House. Gypsy crisscrossed the Atlantic Ocean forty-five times, preaching the gospel to millions of people, and he never preached without someone surrendering their life to the lordship of Jesus Christ.

Gypsy was powerfully used of God. Everywhere he went, it seemed like revival was right on his heels. But it wasn't his preaching that brought revival. It never is. Preaching may move the hearts of men, but praying moves the heart of God. And that's where revival comes from.

Gypsy revealed his secret to a delegation of revival seekers who sought an audience with him. They wanted to know how they could make a difference with their lives the way he had with his. His answer was simple yet profound — as timely and timeless now as it was a hundred years ago. He gave them this advice:

Go home. Lock yourself in your room. Kneel down in the middle of the floor, and with a piece of chalk draw a circle around yourself. There, on your knees, pray fervently and brokenly that God would start a revival within that chalk circle.

Start Circling

I have a confession to make. Even though I wrote a book on prayer, and my personal prayer life was thriving, I failed to lead our church in corporate prayer for fifteen years. That changed this year, and everything changed with it.

We completed our first forty-day prayer challenge at National Community Church, and on a corporate level, it completely changed our church culture. It ranks as the most significant season of spiritual growth in our fifteen-year history. And on a personal level, I'm not who I was when we started.

As we prepared for the forty-day challenge, I believed that God wanted our church to circle 2 Chronicles 7:14 by hitting our knees every day at 7:14 a.m. I explained to our church that the time in and of itself wasn't significant but offered a daily reminder of the promise we were circling in prayer.

> "If my people, who are called by my name, will humble themselves and pray and seek my face and turn from their wicked ways, then I will hear from heaven, and I will forgive their sin and will heal their land."

On the first day of the prayer challenge, I dropped to my knees right after I got out of bed. This daily habit didn't stop on day 40. In fact, I'll do it the rest of my life. Please read this carefully: the goal of the forty-day prayer challenge isn't to get what you want by day 40. In fact, the goal isn't to get what you want at all. The goal is to figure out what God wants, what God wills. Then you start circling it in prayer and don't stop until God answers.

Too often we pray ASAP prayers — *as soon as possible*. We need to start praying ALAT prayers — *as long as it takes*. The goal of the prayer challenge is to establish a prayer habit so you're still praying on day 41, day 57, day 101, day 365.

Logistics

Who should I do the prayer challenge with?

You may want to consider a church-wide challenge or turn

your small group into a prayer circle. You can do this challenge with your family or with your friends. But whatever you do, don't do it alone.

What should I circle?

Don't feel bad if you don't know what to circle on day 1. One of the biggest misconceptions about prayer is that it means outlining our agenda to God as a divine to-do list. The true purpose of prayer is to get into God's presence so He can outline His agenda for us. Here's my advice: pray about what to pray about. God will reveal a promise, a problem, or a person. Then circle whatever God has prompted you to pray for with the same kind of consistency with which the earth circles the sun.

Too often we pray for something once and then completely forget about it. So when God answers, we fail to give Him the glory because we forgot what we asked for. That's one reason why you need to journal during these forty days. Document your prayers and God's answers. If you don't have a journal, pick up a copy of *The Circle Maker Prayer Journal.* It'll help you not just pray, but pray through.

During our forty-day prayer challenge, different people circled different things. We saw prodigals come back to God after years of running away. Marriages were restored. Job opportunities opened up. Provision for financial needs came out of nowhere. Divine appointments happened on a daily basis. And there were even a few miraculous healings.

When should I take the challenge?

You can do this at any time, but the important thing is to establish a start date or end date. A forty-day prayer challenge is a great way to begin a new year or to end a year. At NCC, we approach Lent as a way of beginning the spiritual journey to Easter. This past year, I coined the word *ExperiLent* because we wanted to see what would happen if we circled one promise for forty days, and God delivered. You'll read about it in the devotion for day 34. You can also leverage a birthday or holiday. A forty-day fast leading up to my thirty-fifth birthday was a turning point in my life. I turned my birthday into a self-imposed deadline that yielded my first book.

Where should I pray?

It's important to make a daily appointment with God by determining a *time and place* to pray. If it helps, put the appointment in your calendar or set an alarm. I recommend that you give God the first few minutes of the day. When I pray at the beginning of the day, it's like my whole day becomes a prayer. When I dial into God's frequency in the morning, I hear His still, small voice the rest of the day.

I also recommend a corporate gathering for prayer. Kick it off with a night of prayer and praise. Then sustain the momentum with daily gatherings. Our 7:14 a.m. weekday prayer gatherings not only create tremendous synergy; they also are a way to hold me accountable.

Find Out about Prayer

In 1952, a Princeton doctoral student asked Albert Einstein a question: "What original dissertation research is left?" I'm intrigued and inspired by Einstein's answer: "Find out about prayer."

That is the challenge on the table: find out about prayer.

My prayer for you is that each day on this journey will yield a new discovery. Those discoveries will change the way you pray, and when you change the way you pray, everything else changes.

Few people had a more profound impact on the spiritual climate of America in the last half of the twentieth century than Bill Bright, founder of Campus Crusade for Christ (CRU). He championed evangelism and discipleship from college campuses to foreign mission fields and influenced millions of people through the organization he started and the books he wrote.

In 1994, Dr. Bright felt led to do a forty-day fast for revival in America. The man who went into that prayer circle and the man who came out were two different people. His faith soared. He sensed God's presence like never before. And biblical truths went from his mind to his heart to his soul. In his own words, "This proved to be the most important forty days of my life."

I believe the same thing can be true for you.

Draw the circle!

Get Ready

He prayed to God regularly.
ACTS 10:2

Five words tell me everything I need to know about Cornelius: *He prayed to God regularly.* Scripture doesn't record exactly *when* or *where* or *how* he prayed. It doesn't reveal whether he prayed in the morning or the evening. It doesn't tell us what he said or the posture he prayed in. It just says he prayed regularly. And when you pray to God regularly, irregular things happen on a regular basis. You never know when or where or how God will invade the routine of your life, but you can live in holy anticipation, knowing that God is orchestrating supernatural synchronicities.

Like a grandmaster who strategically positions chess pieces on a chessboard, God is always preparing us and positioning us for divine appointments. And prayer is the way we discern the next move. The plans of God are only revealed in the presence of God. We don't get our marching orders until we get on our knees! But if we hit our knees, God will take us places we never imagined going by paths we didn't even know existed.

If history is a chess match between good and evil, then Acts 10 is one of God's epic moves. It reveals how one prayer can change the game. It reveals what can happen when two people pray. It reveals the power of prayer to checkmate the enemy and seal the victory.

Here's the play-by-play.

A man named Cornelius has a vision while praying in Caesarea. Simultaneously, Peter has a vision while praying in Joppa. Those visions collide in a divine appointment that radically alters the course of history. Up to this point, the Way was a sect of Judaism. It isn't until Cornelius, an officer in the Roman army, puts his faith in Jesus Christ that the gospel is opened up to Gentiles. If *he* doesn't get saved, *you* can't get saved. It's not even an option. So if you're a non-Jewish follower of Jesus, your spiritual genealogy traces back to this genesis moment. When Cornelius puts his faith in Christ, the door of salvation swings wide open to the Gentiles. But it started with two people praying. Those two prayers have been answered billions of times over the last two thousand years. In fact, they were answered yet again when you put your faith in Jesus Christ.

Now let me state the obvious: Cornelius and Peter should have never met each other. Never. Ever. They were separated by geography. The thirty-two-mile distance between their two towns may not seem like much to us, but the average person in the first century didn't travel outside a thirty-mile radius of their birthplace. And more significantly, they were separated by ethnicity. Roman soldiers and Jewish disciples didn't hang out. In fact, Peter broke every law in the Jewish books when he entered the home of Cornelius. Stepping through that doorway was like crossing the Rubicon. He went against everything he'd ever known and risked everything he'd ever accomplished. That doorway to the home of Cornelius was like the wardrobe in *The Lion, the Witch, and the Wardrobe* or the rabbit hole in *Alice in Wonderland*. I call it The Door to Whosoever. When Peter entered the house of Cornelius, it literally meant, "Whosoever will may come." And that includes you and me!

Get Ready

It's not every day that a member of the United States Congress requests a meeting with me. At first I was curious. Then I got a little nervous. I hoped it had nothing to do with the fact that I had illegally taken my kids sledding at the Capitol during snowmaggedon a few winters back, but I figured that couldn't possibly warrant a federal investigation. Turns out the congressman just wanted to thank me for writing *Wild Goose Chase*, a book he read during his first run for Congress.

As we sipped lattes in my office above Ebenezer's Coffeehouse, the congressman shared his backstory with me. Not unlike Daniel's improbable rise to political power, Jim's path was full of unpredictable twists and turns. It all started one day in 2007 when the Holy Spirit said in that still, small voice, "Get ready." His initial reaction was, *Get ready for what?* At the time, Jim was directing one of the largest Christian camps in the country and preaching on weekends. He was perfectly content doing what he was doing, but the Holy Spirit kept impressing the same thing on him: "Get ready."

Several months later, Jim was reading the newspaper when he came across an article about the congresswoman who represented his district. Rumors were flying that she was going to make a run for governor, which would leave her seat in Congress vacant. That's when the Holy Spirit said, "This is it."

Jim didn't have a political bone in his body. In fact, he didn't even know the boundaries of his congressional district. He went online to do a little research when his wife walked in and said, "What are you looking at?" He said, "County statistics." She said, "We're running for Congress, aren't we?" They had never talked about it or thought about it. Running for Congress seemed like a wild goose chase. After all, Jim had no background, no network, and no resources. There was no way he could win — unless, of course, the front-runner happened to drop out of the race a few months before the election. That is exactly what happened, and Jim Lankford was elected to represent the 5th Congressional District of Oklahoma.

The Celtic Christians had a fascinating name for the Holy Spirit. They called Him *An-Geadh-Glas*, which means "wild goose." Can you think of a better description of what it's like to live a Spirit-led life than "wild goose chase"? When you follow the leading of the Holy Spirit, you never know who you'll meet, where you'll go, or what you'll do. But one thing is certain: it'll be anything but boring!

At the end of our conversation, Congressman Lankford mentioned that he had also read *The Circle Maker*. And he's putting it into practice. If you visit the Cannon House Office Building on any given morning when Congress is in session, you'll find a camp-director-turned-congressman circling the fifth floor, praying for his constituents, colleagues, and country!

Anything but Routine

If you establish a prayer routine, your life will be anything but routine. You will go to places, do things, and meet people you have no business going to, doing, or meeting. You don't need to seek opportunity. All you have to do is seek God. And if you seek God, opportunity will seek you.

I live in a town, Washington, D.C., where it's all about who you know. *Who you know* is more important than *what you know*. This is certainly true for the children of God. Who you know — the heavenly Father — is far more important than what you know.

Don't worry about meeting the right people. If you meet with God, God will make sure you meet the right people at the right time. After all, there is nobody He doesn't know. It's one degree of separation! And if God can change the heart of Pharaoh, He can help you find favor with anybody and everybody. Let God do the promoting and networking. I'm certainly not suggesting that you don't apply for a promotion or trade business cards, but seek first His kingdom. You've got to do God's will God's way.

Remember when Moses got impatient and took matters into his own hands by killing an Egyptian taskmaster? He thought it would expedite God's plan. In reality, it delayed God's plan by forty years. He thought it would bring relief, but it made the burden on the Israelites almost unbearable. That's what happens when we try to do God's job for Him. It's unbearable. When we try to make things go faster, we usually slow things down. When we try to make things easier, we usually make them harder.

Don't try to manufacture your own miracles.

Don't try to answer your own prayers.

Don't try to do God's job for Him.

Stay humble. Stay patient. Stay focused.

Keep circling.

 *If you pray to God regularly, irregular things will happen on a regular basis.*

Established by God

In their hearts humans plan their course,
but the LORD establishes their steps.

PROVERBS 16:9

It may feel like you are sitting still right now, but you are not. You are on a planet that is rotating on its axis at 1,000 miles per hour. Like clockwork, it makes one full revolution every twenty-four hours. And if that isn't amazing enough, planet Earth is moving around the sun at speeds approaching 67,000 miles per hour! So the next time you feel like you've had an unproductive day, remind yourself that you did travel more than 1.5 million miles through space today.

Now let me ask you a question: When was the last time you lost sleep because you were concerned about the Creator keeping the planets in orbit? When was the last time you got down on your knees at night and prayed, "Lord, thanks for keeping the planet rotating. I wasn't sure if we'd make the full rotation today, but You did it again!" I'm guessing the answer to these questions is *never*.

We don't doubt God's ability to keep the planets in orbit, but we have a difficult time believing He can keep our lives in orbit. You tell me which is more difficult — keeping the planets in orbit or determining our steps? The truth is that we already trust God for the big things; now we need to trust Him for the little things, like healing our cancer, getting us out of debt, helping us conceive, or helping us find our soul mate. I'm certainly not suggesting that any of these situations are small. They are giant mountains to us. But prayer can turn them into molehills!

God is great not just because nothing is too big for Him; God is also great because nothing is too small. The Sovereign One cares about every minute detail of our lives.

Every act of obedience, no matter how small, makes our heavenly Father proud. Every act of faith — even a faith as small as a mustard seed — puts a smile on His face. Every sacrifice, no matter how insignificant it may seem to us, makes a difference.

Like a proud parent watching their child take their first steps, God rejoices over every baby step. And He can turn those small steps of faith into giant leaps.

Divine Assignment

I have a handful of prayers I pray all the time. Because of their frequent repetition, I call them prayer mantras. One is that God will put my books into the right hands at the right time. I've prayed this prayer thousands of times, and God has answered it in dramatic fashion countless times. The right book in the right hands at the right time can save a marriage, avert a mistake, demand a decision, plant a seed, conceive a dream, solve a problem, and prompt a prayer. That's why I write. And that's why, for me, a book sold is not a book sold; a book sold is a prayer answered. I don't know the name and situation of every reader, but God does, and that's all that matters.

The other day I got an e-mail from Peter, a man who started reading *In a Pit with a Lion on a Snowy Day* on a flight to Las Vegas. During the first half of his flight, he read chapter 1 and felt challenged and convicted. One sentence arrested his attention: "God is in the business of strategically positioning us in the right place at the right time, but it's up to us to see and seize those opportunities that are all around us all the time." So Peter switched planes in Phoenix and sat down in his new seat assignment. He said hello to the girl next to him, but she shut him down rather abruptly. It was one of those looks that says, *Don't talk to me the rest of this flight, and by the way, the armrest belongs to me!* Peter didn't want to offend her or bother her, but he couldn't shake the feeling that something was wrong. He knew he needed to swallow his pride, face his fears, and seize the opportunity. He leaned over and said, "I know it's absolutely none of my business, but you seem so burdened. If sharing it with a complete stranger might help, I'm all ears."

The seventeen-year-old girl, who was three months pregnant, proceeded to tell him she was running away from home. Her boyfriend told her to take off and "take care of it." She had stolen her dad's credit card that morning to buy a ticket to Vegas to get an abortion. During the flight, Peter spoke words of comfort and encouragement. When they landed in

Vegas, he convinced the girl to call her parents, who were worried sick. Her parents convinced her to grab the next flight and come home.

I'm quite sure one life, perhaps two, were saved that day! All because one man believed that a seat assignment might be a divine assignment. And when we act on those prayer promptings, the Grandmaster can use a single pawn to checkmate the enemy's plans.

At the end of his e-mail, Peter thanked me for writing the book. He wrote, "So that's what happened after chapter 1. I can't wait to see what happens after chapter 2!" Me too! All I know is this: God is setting up divine appointments all the time. Only God can *make* the appointment, but only you can *keep* the appointment. It's your job to recognize and respond to the God-ordained opportunities that come your way.

Choreography

Few promises are more circled in my Bible than Proverbs 16:9: "In their hearts humans plan their course, but the LORD establishes their steps."

God wants us to get where God wants us to go more than we want to get where God wants us to go. And He is awfully good at getting us there. All we have to do is follow the script of Holy Scripture and the improvisation of the Holy Spirit.

We can't create divine appointments. All we can do is keep them.

We can't plan God-ordained opportunities. All we can do is seize them.

We can't perform miracles. All we can do is pray for them.

Our job is to hear His voice. His job is to establish our steps. And if we do our job, God will do His!

The Hebrew word *kûn*, translated in Proverbs 16:9 as "establishes," can also be translated as "determines," "prepares," "provides," "sets in place," "directs," "firmly decides," "makes secure." It's a meticulous word that involves careful planning right down to the smallest detail. It's a redemptive word that celebrates God's ability to redeem past experiences and recycle them for future opportunities. It's a calming word that imparts confidence in the fact that God has everything under control. It's a creative word that hints at the beauty of God's artistry.

God is the Composer. Your life is His musical score.

God is the Artist. Your life is His canvas.

God is the Architect. Your life is His blueprint.

God is the Writer. You are His book.

God is great not just because nothing is too big for Him; God is also great because nothing is too small.

Amazing Things

*"Consecrate yourselves, for tomorrow
the LORD will do amazing things among you."*
JOSHUA 3:5

More than a hundred years ago, a British revivalist spoke the words to Dwight L. Moody that would transform Moody's approach to life — words of challenge that echo across every generation: "The world has yet to see what God will do with and for and through and in and by the man who is fully and wholly consecrated to Him."

Why not you?

All of us want to do amazing things for God, but that isn't our job; it is God's job. Our job is simply to consecrate ourselves by yielding our will to His will. And if we do our job, God will do His job. If we consecrate ourselves to God, amazing things will happen. It's absolutely inevitable. Consecration always ends in amazing!

The Israelites were camped on the eastern banks of the Jordan River when God gave them this command: "Consecrate yourselves." And because they obeyed, God delivered on the promise. He parted the Jordan River, and the Israelites walked through on dry ground. We'd rather build a boat or build a bridge. We try to do things for God instead of letting God do things for us. And it's certainly a two-way street. We need to *work like it depends on us*, but we also need to *pray like it depends on God*. That's what consecration is all about. It's letting God do for us what we cannot do for ourselves. And that's how God gets all the glory.

Consecration is a complete surrender to the lordship of Jesus Christ. We relinquish everything to God — our time, talent, and treasure. It's a complete divestiture. Nothing belongs to us, not even ourselves. But the exchange rate is unbelievable. All of our sin is transferred to Christ's account, and all of His righteousness is transferred to our account. God cancels our debt, writes us into His will, and calls it even!

The word *consecrate* means "to set apart." It means "to be designated for a special purpose." It means "to be completely dedicated to God."

The Son of God set the standard. Jesus gave all of Himself at Calvary, and He expects nothing less in return. If Jesus hung on His cross, we can certainly carry our cross. His death demands our lives.

Gate D8

During our prayer challenge at National Community Church, our church gathered for corporate prayer every morning at our coffeehouse. Like clockwork, we hit our knees at 7:14 a.m. sharp. It was such a regular routine that it became second nature. Almost like hunger pangs that hit you after going too long without eating, I couldn't go too long without hitting my knees. Kneeling became almost as instinctual as eating or sleeping.

One day I had to miss our prayer meeting because of an early morning flight to Cleveland. As I got off the plane, I realized it was time to pray. I knew I'd be kneeling at our coffeehouse, but I was in the middle of an airport. And that's when I felt the Holy Spirit throwing down the gauntlet, impressing on me the need to kneel right then and there. To be honest, I resisted: "But, Lord, I'm in the middle of the Cleveland airport." The Lord said, "I know exactly where you are. Gate D8."

At first I rationalized *not* kneeling.

I don't want to feed negative stereotypes about religious fanatics. I can pray just as effectively as I walk toward baggage claim. I can kneel a little later in the privacy of my hotel room.

While all of these things are true, I knew it wasn't the point. I knew the Lord was testing me to see if I'd be willing to obey Him whenever, wherever, whatever. I knew that if I failed this test, I would be standing in God's way of using me in bigger ways. I wanted to prove to Him that I cared more about what He thought than about what people thought. I wanted to prove to Him that I belong to Him everywhere, all the time. And I knew that if God could trust me with the little things, then He could use me to do big things. So after looking both ways down the terminal, I hit my knees at Gate D8. It was one small step in the long journey toward complete consecration. A little piece of my ego died that day at Gate D8.

I shared that story with our congregation, and I was inspired by the response. You've heard of a flash mob? Well, our church became a kneeling mob! I've heard stories of people kneeling in elevators, in classrooms, in banks, and in courtrooms. It isn't about kneeling in strange places at strange times; it's about the willingness to obey the promptings of the Holy Spirit. It's about a willingness to kneel anyplace, anytime.

Veto Power

Consecration means we no longer call the shots. We give God veto power. His word is the final word, whether it's Holy Scripture or the Holy Spirit. Either way, it's no longer a selfish spirituality that asks God to serve our purposes. It's all about serving His purposes so that His glory is revealed.

Consecration is death to self.

I know there is a fear that if we give more of ourselves to God, there will be less of us left, but it's the exact opposite. It's not until we die to self that we truly come alive. The more we give to God, the more we have and the more we become. It's only in losing our lives that we will really find them.

Sometimes prayer is a casual conversation with God. It's like two friends catching up over coffee. But sometimes prayer involves intense intercession, as it was for Jesus praying in Gethsemane on the eve of His crucifixion. It was so intense that Jesus was literally sweating drops of blood. He was facing the greatest test of his life on earth, so He prayed through the night. Three times He prayed a prayer of consecration: "My

Father, if it is possible, may this cup be taken from me. Yet not as I will, but as you will."

Consecration is a process of surrender that never ends. And prayer is the catalyst. It begins with a sinner's prayer. We confess our sins to the Savior and surrender our lives to His lordship. And along the way, our spiritual journeys are marked by decisive moments when we consecrate ourselves to God in our own garden of Gethsemane.

Jonathan Edwards is famous for his sermon "Sinners in the Hands of an Angry God," which helped spark the first Great Awakening. Along with his pastorate in North Hampton, Massachusetts, he served as the president of Princeton University. Of his known descendants, there are more than 300 ministers or missionaries, 120 university professors, 60 authors, 30 judges, 14 college presidents, 3 members of Congress, and 1 vice president. That's an impressive family lineage! And that legacy, like every spiritual genealogy, traces back to a moment of consecration.

On January 12, 1723, Jonathan Edwards made a solemn dedication of himself to God. He consecrated himself, all of himself, to God.

> I made a solemn dedication of myself to God, and wrote it down; giving up myself, and all that I had to God; to be for the future, in no respect, my own; to act as one that had no right to himself, in any respect. And solemnly vowed, to take God for my whole portion and felicity; looking on nothing else, as any part of my happiness, nor acting as if it were.

If we give more of ourselves to God,
God will give more of Himself to us.

Don't Pray Away

"This happened so that the works of God might be displayed in him."
JOHN 9:3

My friends John and Tricia Tiller experienced a parent's worst nightmare nearly a decade ago. Their three-year-old son, Eli, was playing by himself in his room when Tricia became concerned because it was too quiet. When she walked into his room, Eli was nowhere to be seen. That's when she saw a table out of place. It had been pushed beneath his second-story bedroom window, and the window screen was conspicuously missing. Tricia's worst fears were realized when she ran to the window, looked down, and saw Eli lying thirteen feet below.

Eli was medivaced to the hospital, where he fought for his life in the ICU for three weeks. He miraculously survived, but not without significant brain damage. He has virtually no peripheral vision on his right side, and the left side of his body has very little motor skills or muscle development. Eli speaks with a severe stutter and walks with a pronounced limp. Yet twelve-year-old Eli Tiller has as sweet a spirit and as courageous an attitude as anybody I've ever met. He recently sang at National Community Church, and there wasn't a dry eye in the place.

John and Tricia have thanked God countless times for saving their son, but their prayers for complete healing have gone unanswered. In the aftermath of the accident, John dueled with doubt.

I began to interrogate God. "Why, God? Why do little boys fall from windows?"

Why did my little boy fall from that window? Why him? Why me? I looked to Scripture for an answer, and it turns out that "Why, God?" is not a new question at all.

In John 9, Jesus encountered a man who was born blind, and the people falsely assumed it was the result of sin. They asked Jesus, "Who sinned, this man or his parents?" Jesus told them it was neither! The people assumed it was a generational curse or a lack of faith. But Jesus set the record straight by revealing the real reason: "This happened so that the works of God might be displayed in him."

Since Eli's accident, Tricia and I have done everything humanly possible to make our son well. We've spent tens of thousands of dollars on uninsured medical equipment. For the first three years after the accident, Tricia and Eli literally spent 80 percent of their waking hours in therapy. We had faith that he would be completely healed. We knew it was going to happen, so we just kept praying and kept waiting. We waited and waited. We knew that one day we'd be standing in front of crowds saying, "Look what the Lord has done! He has completely healed our son." But that's not what happened.

After three years of doing everything we could for our son, it was time to accept his current condition and choose to live life with disability. This disability was something we couldn't remove, and evidently God was choosing to not completely heal Eli. So we had to burn our old scripts and look for what God could do with our new script. So for the past five years, we've accepted life with disability. That doesn't mean I've stopped praying for my son. Like any father, I'd give my right arm to see my son healed. But instead of getting discouraged or getting angry, I choose to look for what God can do.

Sometimes the purpose of prayer is to *get us out of* circumstances, but more often than not, the purpose of prayer is to *get us through* them. I'm certainly not suggesting we shouldn't pray deliverance prayers, but there are times we need to pray prevailing prayers. We need to ask God to give us the grace to sustain, the strength to stand firm, and the willpower to keep on keeping on.

Praying Away versus Praying Through

There is a big difference between *praying away* and *praying through*.

We're often so anxious to get out of difficult, painful, or challenging situations that we fail to grow through them. We're so fixated on *getting out of them* that we don't *get anything out of them*. We fail to learn the lessons God is trying to teach us or cultivate the character God is trying to grow in us. We're so focused on God changing our circumstances that we never allow God to change us! So instead of ten or twenty years of experience, we have one year of experience repeated ten or twenty times.

Sometimes we need to pray "get me out" prayers. But sometimes we need to pray "get me through" prayers. And we need the discernment to know when to pray what.

If we're being completely honest, most of our prayers have as their chief objective our own personal comfort rather than God's glory. We want to pray away every problem, but those shortsighted prayers would short-circuit God's perfect plan. There are seasons and situations when we need to simply pray through.

My prayer batting average is no better than anyone else's. I swing and miss all the time, but I have determined that I'm going to "go down swinging." Even when a prayer isn't answered the way I want, I have a peace that passes understanding because I know that God heard me. It just means the answer is no. And I've learned to praise God when the answer is no, not just when the answer is yes. It simply means I'm asking for the wrong thing or for the wrong reason or at the wrong time. And I'm convinced that the day will come when we thank God for the prayers He did *not* answer as much as the ones He did because He had a better answer. And the best answer is very rarely what is most convenient or comfortable for us. The best answer is always what brings God the most glory!

Can our prayers change our circumstances? Absolutely! But when our circumstances don't change, it's often an indication that God is trying to change us. The primary purpose of prayer is not to change circumstances; the primary purpose of prayer is to change us! But either way, the chief objective remains the same: to glorify God in any and every situation.

Sometimes God delivers us from our problems; sometimes God delivers us through our problems.

Write It Down

"Write down the revelation."
HABAKKUK 2:2

I have a handful of sayings that our staff can recite from memory because I repeat them all the time. One of them is this: *the shortest pencil is longer than the longest memory.* That's why I keep a prayer journal. Next to my Bible, nothing is more sacred to me than my journal. It's the way I mark my trail. It's the way I process problems and record revelations. It's the way I keep track of the prayers I've prayed so that I can give God the glory when He answers.

Journaling is one of the most overlooked and undervalued spiritual disciplines. In my estimation, it's on a par with praying, fasting, and meditating. It's the way we document what God is doing in our lives. In Habakkuk 2:2, the Lord states, "Write down the revelation." Why? Because we have a natural tendency to remember what we should forget and forget what we should remember. Journaling is the best antidote, maybe the only antidote, to spiritual amnesia.

This year I started taking my journal with me everywhere I go. When I'm in a meeting, I write things in my prayer journal so I can double back and pray about them later. If I'm listening to someone speak, I take notes so I can process them in prayer. And of course, I always have my prayer journal handy when I'm praying. I pray about current situations and future dreams. I have a prayer list for my children that helps me pray consistently and strategically. And I often journal my meditations on Scripture. Then, every once in a while, I go back through my journal and circle the things I need to keep praying through.

My prayer journal doubles as my prayer genealogy. I can trace many of the blessings, breakthroughs, and miracles back to their genesis prayers. As I look back through my journals, I'm able to connect the dots between my prayers and God's answers. Connecting these dots inspires my faith like nothing else because it paints a picture of God's faithfulness.

We kicked off this calendar year with a sermon series on *The Circle Maker*, and I encouraged everyone in our congregation to get a prayer journal. I've been amazed at how many people's prayer lives have been revolutionized by the simple act of journaling. I'm convinced it is the key to consistency and specificity in prayer. And it even adds an element of fun. It turns prayer into a game of watching and waiting to see how God will answer!

Journal like a Journalist

One of our church attenders recently shared with me one of the most well-documented prayer testimonies I've ever received. It seems particularly appropriate that this testament to journaling came from a journalist. After I read it, this thought fired across my synapses: we all need to journal like a journalist.

Kimberly's lifelong dream was to work at a major network covering politics. Not only did she end up at the largest network; she got to cover the most famous address in the country, 1600 Pennsylvania Avenue. As a member of the White House travel pool, she often accompanies the president on Air Force One. In fact, her first trip was April 29, 2011 — the same day that President Obama authorized the Osama bin Laden mission.

Kimberly is living her dream, but like every dream, it took a lot of prayer and a lot of patience. During our sermon series on *The Circle Maker*, she went back through dozens of her journals from the past decade. As she retraced her steps, she saw the hand of God on every page. Kimberly's prayer genealogy started in 2001. As a college senior, she penned this fragile yet faith-filled prayer:

> *Dare I ask for my dreams? Dare I see the imagination of the soul? Dare I risk? What if I ask and receive? So then, I risk. I ask of my King, "May I impact others with news and knowledge?"*

After college, Kimberly thought about grad school, considered pursuing library science, and contemplated moving to Chicago or New York. It was during this season of wandering that she created a prayer map — a sheet of paper in her journal with a verse at the top and prayer requests written below. On one of those pages, she circled Psalm 37:4: "Delight yourself in the LORD; and He will give you the desires of your heart." That was a critical promise at a critical time.

On November 4, 2003, she wrote out this prayer:

Where do you want me to go? Where can I represent you? Where is your will? Tug at my heart. I am willing and waiting.

Fast-forward to April 15, 2004.

Kimberly was sitting on a bench overlooking Lake Michigan, depressed by how much money she wasn't making. In that moment, the dream of working at a major network was birthed in her spirit. She also knew she needed to take a step of faith and move to Washington, D.C. So with no job and very little money, Kimberly made the move to D.C. She slept on a friend's floor for several months until she could get on her feet financially. To make ends meet, she worked for a temp agency filing papers while she sent out hundreds of résumés and made hundreds of cold calls.

After numerous dead ends, Kimberly finally got her first break working for a small news bureau during the graveyard shift. Her first night as a full-time journalist was the day Hurricane Katrina hit.

As awful as those overnights were, turns out those overnights were the best thing to hone my journalistic skills. This was also the height of the Iraq War so everything was happening overnight. I got to see how the early morning shift can set the agenda for the entire news cycle.

About a year into the overnight shift, Kimberly wanted to

get a day job so she could get a life! It was killing her social life and spiritual life, so she applied for a day job with a major network. She thought her dream job was finally at her fingertips. She got an interview, but the door slammed shut. It was devastating. That's when many of us give up on our dreams, but Kimberly kept circling her dream job while working her night job for another year! Then she got another interview with the same network, and this time the door opened.

Long story short, it took a decade of working like it depended on her and praying like it depended on God for her dream to come true. But because she journaled her prayers, Kimberly is able to look back and see how God determined her steps. God's fingerprints were on every page!

I'm the granddaughter of farmers. One of my grandmothers only got an eighth-grade education because she had to leave school to help out on the farm. She was told, "All you'll ever do is milk cows."

Now her granddaughter works at the White House. She can be in the Oval Office and say, "Excuse me, Mr. President."

What a country. What a God.

Draw the Circle

The shortest pencil is longer than the longest memory.

Shameless Audacity

"... yet because of your shameless audacity
he will surely get up and give you
as much as you need."

LUKE 11:8

I was doing a radio interview shortly after *The Circle Maker* was released, and the host of the show told an amazing story about his missionary friend, Dr. Bob Bagley. Bob's church in Africa didn't have a church building, so they literally met under the shade of a single tree near the village — that is, until the local witch doctor cursed the tree, and it withered. The church didn't just lose their shade; they were overshadowed by the curse. It undermined the authority of their message. Bob knew their status in the village was in jeopardy if he didn't do something about it, so he called for a public prayer meeting. Not unlike Elijah, who challenged the prophets of Baal to a prayer duel, Bob confronted the curse and called down a blessing on the tree. He literally laid hands on the tree and prayed that God would resurrect it.

Now *that's* shameless audacity!

If God doesn't answer his prayer, he would have dug an

even deeper hole. That is the risk of prayer, isn't it? But if we don't ask, we'll never know. We accumulate lots of wouldas, couldas, and shouldas. Here's what I know for sure: God won't answer 100 percent of the prayers we don't pray.

There is an old adage: *Desperate times call for desperate measures*. Every prayer is a calculated risk, but sometimes God calls us to ante up all the faith we have, and then let the chips fall where they may! That's what Bob did. He asked God to resurrect a tree, and then he added a little tagline to his prayer: "It's not my name that's at stake."

When we act in faith, we aren't risking our reputation; we are risking God's reputation because He's the one who made the promise in the first place. But if we aren't willing to risk our reputation, we'll never establish God's reputation. We'll also never experience miracles like the one Bob saw. Not only did God break the curse and resurrect the tree; it became the only tree of its type to yield its fruit, not once, but twice a year. A double crop! A double blessing!

Why do we mistakenly think that God is offended by our prayers for the impossible? The truth is that God is offended by anything less! God is offended when we ask Him to do things we can do ourselves. It's the impossible prayers that honor God because they reveal our faith and allow God to reveal His glory.

Shameless Audacity

In Luke 11, Jesus tells a story about a man who won't take no for an answer. He keeps knocking on his friend's door until he gets what he came for. It's a parable about prevailing in prayer. And Jesus honors his bold determination: "... yet because of your shameless audacity he will surely get up and give you as much as you need."

I love this depiction of prayer. There are times when you need to do whatever it takes. You need to grab hold of the horns of the altar and not let go. You need to dare demonic forces to a duel. You need to do something crazy, something risky, something different.

The epitome of shameless audacity is the circle maker himself. When a severe drought threatened to destroy a generation of Jews, Honi drew a circle in the sand, dropped to his knees, and said, "Lord of the universe, I swear before Your great name that I will not move from this circle until You have shown mercy upon Your children."

It was a risky proposition. Honi could have been in that circle a long time! But God honored that bold prayer because that bold prayer honored Him. And even when God answered that prayer for rain, Honi had the shameless audacity to ask for a specific type of rain. "Not for such rain have I prayed, but for rain of Your favor, blessing, and graciousness."

The moral of this parable is to prevail in prayer, but it also reveals the character of Him who answers prayer. The request is *not* granted simply because of repeated requests. Prayer is answered to preserve God's good name. After all, it's not our reputation that is on the line; it's His reputation. So God doesn't answer prayer just to give us what we want; God answers prayer to bring glory to His name.

The beauty of obedience is this: it relieves us of responsibility. It takes all the pressure off of us and places it squarely on God's sovereign shoulders.

When we give God the tithe, for example, our finances are no longer our responsibility; they become God's responsibility. God even says, "Test me in this." And if we test God, we'll find that He can do more with 90 percent than we can do with 100 percent. It turns financial management into a giving game that gets more fun the more we give. And the more we give away, the more we can enjoy what we keep.

When we pray, we relieve ourselves of responsibility. We let go and let God. We take our hands off and put our concerns into the hands of Almighty God. And trust me, He can handle whatever we put in His hands.

Sometimes we're afraid of praying for miracles because we're afraid that God won't answer, but the answer isn't up to us. We never know if the answer will be yes, no, or not yet. But the answer isn't up to us. It's not our job to answer; it's our job to ask. And Jesus exhorts us to ask.

> "Ask and it will be given to you; seek and you will find; knock and the door will be opened to you."

These three words — *ask*, *seek*, and *knock* — are present imperative verbs. In other words, they aren't something we do once; they are actions that are repeated over and over and over again.

Keep asking. Keep seeking. Keep knocking.

And, I might add, keep circling.

The greatest tragedy in life
is the prayers that go unanswered
simply because they go unasked.

Put on Waders

They went forth and preached every where, the Lord ...
confirming the word with signs following.
MARK 16:20 KJV

The first testimony I received after writing *The Circle Maker* — and one of my favorites — made reference to a drought in Mississippi fifty years ago. Not unlike Honi the circle maker, whose prayer ended a first-century drought in Israel, one man's faith rose to the occasion in the land of the Delta.

When a drought threatened to destroy a season of crops, a rural church with many farmers in the congregation called for an emergency prayer meeting. Dozens of farmers showed up to pray. Most of them wore their traditional overalls, but one of them wore waders! He got a few funny looks, just like Noah did when he was building the ark, but isn't that faith at its finest? If we genuinely believe God is going to answer our prayer for rain, isn't that exactly what we would wear? Why not dress for the miracle? I love the simple, childlike faith of that old, seasoned farmer. He simply said, "I don't want to walk home wet." And he didn't. But everyone else did.

I can't help but wonder if that act of faith is what sealed the miracle. I don't know for sure, but this I do know: God is honored when we act *as if* He is going to answer our prayers! And acting *as if* means acting on our prayers. After hitting our knees, we need to take a small step of faith. And those small steps of faith often turn into giant leaps.

Like Noah, who kept building an ark day after day, we keep hammering away at the dream God has given us. Like the Israelites, who kept circling Jericho for seven days, we keep circling God's promises. Like Elijah, who kept sending his servant back to look for a rain cloud, we actively and expectantly wait for God's answer.

$85 Faith

A year before we purchased the old crack house on Capitol Hill that we turned into Ebenezer's Coffeehouse, I took an $85 step of faith. And I believe this $85 step of faith set us up for the $3 million miracle that happened many years later.

I was at an auction where items were being sold off to benefit our children's school. Most people were bidding on class projects or tickets to sporting events or vacations. Not me. I had my eye on one item: a book on Capitol Hill zoning codes donated by the Capitol Hill Restoration Society.

I knew I could buy a copy for less money *after* we got a contract on the property, but I felt I needed to demonstrate my faith and purchase it *before* we got the contract. If we weren't able to get the property, it would be a complete waste of money. But I believed that God was going to give it to us, so I acted on it by making an $85 bid. I got the book, and a few months later we got the contract on the property.

Sometimes we need to take an $85 step of faith just to show God that we're serious. It proves our faith.

Don't just pray about your dream; act on it. Act *as if* God is going to deliver on His promise. Maybe it's time to put on waders and act as if God is going to answer. Maybe it's time to make an $85 down payment on your dream.

Buy a ticket to the Broadway show you're auditioning for. Buy a new suit for the dream job you've applied for. Buy a piece of furniture for the dream home you've been saving for. Buy a share of stock. Buy a subscription. Buy a book.

This isn't some "name it, claim it" scheme. If it's not in the will of God, if it's not for the glory of God, it's a waste of time, energy, and money. But if the dream is ordained by God, then that $85 step of faith honors God. And God will honor your $85 faith. Think of it as a down payment on your dream.

Signs Following

The last two words of Mark's gospel are "signs following."

We wish it said "signs preceding."

We want God to go first. That way we don't need to exercise any faith at all. But we've got it backward. If we want to see God move, we need to make a move. If it seems like God isn't moving in our lives, maybe it's because we aren't moving. But if we make a move, God will move heaven and earth to honor our faith.

There comes a moment when we need to make a statement

of faith. I'm not talking about a collection of theological truths written on paper; I'm talking about a statement of faith written with our lives. *Faith* is not a noun; it's a verb — an action verb. The greatest and truest statement of faith is a life well lived. It is faith fleshed out through risks and sacrifices. It is daring to go after a dream that is destined to fail without divine intervention.

We can pray until our knees are numb, but if our praying isn't accompanied by acting, then we won't get anywhere. We need to put feet to our faith. After kneeling down, we need to stand up and step out in faith. There is an old adage: *the journey of a thousand miles begins with the first step*. Based on my experience, that first step is always the hardest and longest step. It will require the most faith. It will feel the most awkward. But if we step out in faith, signs will follow. In fact, an avalanche of blessing will overtake us and overwhelm us. We'll be buried in God's blessings.

Wet Feet

When the Israelites were on the verge of entering the Promised Land, God commanded the priests to step into the river. It's one of the most counterintuitive commands in Scripture: "When you reach the banks of the Jordan River, take a few steps into the river."

I don't know about you, but I don't particularly like getting my feet wet. I'd much rather have God part the river, and then I'll step into the miracle. That way I don't get my feet wet, but if we aren't willing to get our feet wet, we'll never walk through parted rivers on dry ground.

At flood tide, the Jordan River was approximately two hundred feet wide. That was all that separated the Israelites from their four-hundred-year-old promise. Their dream was practically a stone's throw away. But if the priests hadn't stepped into the river, they may well have spent the rest of their lives on the eastern banks of the Jordan River. And that's where many of us spend our lives. We're so close to the dream, so close to the promise, so close to the miracle. But we're waiting for God to part the river, while God is waiting for us to get our feet wet.

We'll never see God part the Jordan River if our feet are firmly planted on dry ground. But if we step into the river, God will part it.

If you want to see God move,
make a move.

One God-Idea

"Speak to the earth, and it will teach you."
JOB 12:8

Around the turn of the twentieth century, the agricultural economy of the South was suffering as the boll weevil devastated cotton crops. The soil was being depleted of nutrients because farmers planted cotton year in and year out.

Enter George Washington Carver, one of the most brilliant scientific minds of the twentieth century. Carver introduced the concept of crop rotation and encouraged farmers to plant peanuts instead of cotton. The rotation of crops revived the soil, but it didn't revive the economy because there was no market for peanuts. The abundant peanut crop rotted in warehouses because supply was greater than demand. When frustrated farmers complained to Carver, he did what he had always done: he took a long walk and had a long talk with God.

George Washington Carver routinely got up at 4:00 a.m., walked through the woods, and asked God to reveal the mysteries of nature. Job 12:7 – 8 was one of the most-circled promises in his Bible.

> "But ask the animals, and they will teach you,
> or the birds in the sky, and they will tell you;
> or speak to the earth, and it will teach you,
> or let the fish in the sea inform you."

Carver took that promise at face value. He literally asked God to reveal the mysteries of nature. And God answered his prayer. Carver is famous for discovering more than three hundred uses for the peanut, but the genesis of those revelations was one conversation with God. In his own inimitable fashion, Carver shared the story behind the story.

> I asked God, "Why did you make the universe, Lord?"
>
> "Ask for something more in proportion to that little mind of yours," replied God.
>
> "Why did you make the earth, Lord?" I asked.
>
> "Your little mind still wants to know far too much. Ask for something more in proportion to that little mind of yours," replied God.
>
> "Why did you make man, Lord?" I asked.
>
> "Far too much. Far too much. Ask again," replied God.
>
> "Explain to me why you made plants, Lord," I asked.
>
> "Your little mind still wants to know far too much."
>
> "The peanut?" I asked meekly.
>
> "Yes! For your modest proportions, I will grant you the mystery of the peanut. Take it inside your laboratory and separate it into water, fats, oils, gums, resins, sugars, starches, and amino acids. Then recombine these under my three laws of compatibility, temperature, and pressure. Then you will know why I made the peanut."

On January 20, 1921, George Washington Carver testified before the House Ways and Means Committee on behalf of the United Peanut Association of America. The chairman, Joseph Fordney of Michigan, told him he had ten minutes. An hour and forty minutes later, the committee told Carver he could come back whenever he wanted and take as much time as he needed. Carver mesmerized the committee by demonstrating a myriad of ingenious uses for the peanut — everything from glue to shaving cream to soap to insecticide to cosmetics to wood stains to fertilizer to linoleum to Worcestershire sauce.

The next time you shave or put on makeup, the next time you stain the deck or fertilize your garden, the next time you enjoy a good old-fashioned PBJ, remember that all of those things trace back to a man who had a habit of praying at 4:00 a.m.

Those three hundred uses of the peanut were *not* good ideas; they were God-ideas. And one God-idea is worth more than a thousand good ideas.

Good ideas are good, but only God-ideas change the course of history.

God-Ideas

Every year, we have an annual theme at National Community Church. It's not just some catchy phrase that rhymes with the year, like "Learning to Lean in 2013." It's the by-product of pressing into God's presence and discerning what God wants to do in us and through us. The theme this year is simply this: *Get into God's presence.*

That is the solution to every problem. That is the answer to every question.

We don't get a vision from God by going to conferences. We might get some good ideas, but God-ideas are only revealed in the presence of God.

Everyone needs counseling of some sort at some point in their lives, but our biggest problems are only solved in the presence of God.

Go ahead and do a planning meeting. After all, failing to plan is planning to fail. But don't just brainstorm; praystorm. The best plans are birthed in the presence of God.

At some point in our lives, the best we can do isn't good enough. Our best solutions, ideas, and efforts aren't good enough. That's when we need to hit our knees and trust God to do what only God can do. After all, *prayer is the difference between the best you can do and the best God can do.* And that's a big difference!

If we hit our knees, the Holy Spirit will do the heavy lifting. If we hit our knees, the Holy Spirit will reveal things that can only be discovered in the presence of God. If we hit our knees, the Holy Spirit will give us God-ideas for our ministry, family, business — for our lives.

The Solution to 10,000 Problems

The modern mystic A. W. Tozer believed that a low view of God is the cause of a hundred lesser evils, but a high view of God is the solution to ten thousand temporal problems. If that's true, and I believe it is, then your biggest problem isn't an impending divorce or a doctor's diagnosis or a failing business. Please understand, I'm not making light of your relational, financial, or health issues. I certainly don't want to minimize the overwhelming challenges you may be facing. But in order to regain a godly perspective on your problems, you must answer this question: *Are my problems bigger than God, or is God bigger than my problems?*

Our biggest problem is our small view of God. That is the cause of all lesser evils. And a high view of God is the solution to all other problems.

Until we come to the conviction that God's grace and God's power know no limits, we will draw small prayer circles. But once we embrace the omnipotence of God, we'll draw ever-enlarging circles around our God-given, God-sized dreams.

How big is your God?

Is He big enough to heal your marriage or heal your child? Is He bigger than a positive MRI or a negative evaluation? Is He bigger than your worst sin, greatest fear, or biggest dream?

If He is bigger than all of those things, then pray like it.

Draw the Circle

One God-idea is worth more than a thousand good ideas.

Dream Factory

We take captive every thought
to make it obedient to Christ.
2 CORINTHIANS 10:5

I have a friend who is out to change the world, one mal-nourished child at a time.

In fall 2008, Mark Moore was working on Capitol Hill after spending ten years in Africa as a missionary. That's when a briefing from a UNICEF representative changed the trajectory of his life. The rep shared about a revolutionary food supplement called RUTF — Ready-to-Use Therapeutic Food — and showed a *60 Minutes* clip featuring Anderson Cooper, who called it "the most important advance ever to cure and treat malnutrition." For Mark, discovering RUTF was like discovering the cure for cancer. It was more than a good idea; he knew it was a God-idea.

The primary ingredient in RUTF is peanut paste. Peanuts are high in calories and rich in proteins, which support the immune system. And the combination of vitamins and minerals are easily digestible for those whose stomachs have shrunk because of malnutrition. It's the perfect food, the miracle food.

I'm not sure George Washington Carver knew that peanut paste would become the single greatest weapon in the fight against malnutrition, but God knew. And the revelation that saved the agricultural economy of the South a hundred years ago has the potential to save millions of lives today. That is the potential of one God-idea. That is the by-product of one prayer.

On October 16, 2009, Mark launched MANA, which stands for Mother Administered Nutritive Aid. But the acronym is really a double entendre. Like the manna that God provided for the Israelites in the wilderness, it's a miracle for those who receive it!

After stepping into the Jordan River and launching MANA, Mark set out to build a facility that could produce mass quantities of RUTF at cheap prices — but he knew God would have to part the waters. He targeted Georgia since it was the peanut capital of the country, and he identified a town called Fitzgerald. When he shared the vision of MANA with the mayor, the mayor said he'd do everything in his power to facilitate and expedite the building permits if Mark could raise $1 million. One trip to Houston, and one angel donor, took care of the $1 million. And within two weeks, they broke ground on a 30,000 square-foot facility that can produce up to 18,000 packets of RUTF every hour. Last month, MANA produced more than one million lifesaving packets!

Dream Factory

Now here's the rest of the story.

Not long after this God-idea got into his spirit, Mark sent

me an e-mail with the subject line "A Million Lives Saved at Ebenezer's." That got my attention! Mark explained that the vision for MANA was conceived at our coffeehouse. And the official launch, which took place on World Food Day, happened at Ebenezer's as well. So I felt like an accomplice to a holy conspiracy.

Then I remembered a prayer we had prayed many years before. And I connected the dots between that prophetic prayer and its fulfillment.

On March 13, 2006, we dedicated Ebenezer's Coffeehouse to the Lord. We laid hands on the walls, wrote prayers on the floors, and prayed for every person who would walk through our doors — which would have included Mark.

The most memorable moment, however, was when one of our staff members specifically prayed that Ebenezer's would be a *dream factory*. It was one of those moments when you almost open your eyes during prayer to see if it impacted everyone else the same way. It was a specific prayer, a prophetic prayer. This one prayer has been answered hundreds of times since it was first prayed. And Mark is an example of how God can answer one prayer in a way that will affect millions of lives. This is what Mark wrote:

> *The dream of MANA was formed in the dream factory of Ebenezer's Coffeehouse. Its great coffee and free Wi-Fi made for the perfect office. As that dream began to gel and I began to pull together resources and relationships to pursue the dream, Ebenezer's became the meeting place. Meeting after meeting occurred there. Many were planned and scheduled, as in "meet me at Ebenezer's at 2:00 p.m.," but many more*

happened by accident. Those meetings led to new ideas, new partnerships, new opportunities, and new relationships that eventually brought us to where we are today.

Severe acute malnutrition will not be stopped by one organization putting peanut paste in a pouch, but we can launch the greatest attack ever on malnutrition and the needless death it brings.

This idea, conceived in Mark's spirit at Ebenezer's Coffeehouse, was more than a good idea; it was a God-idea. And when you get a God-idea, you need to take it captive. In the words of Paul, "Take captive every thought to make it obedient to Christ."

Growing up, I consistently heard this verse interpreted in negative terms. Take captive sinful thoughts and make them obedient to Christ. And that is half the battle. But if we see only the negative implications and not the positive possibilities, it becomes a half-truth. This verse is not just about capturing sinful thoughts and getting them out of our minds; it's also about capturing creative thoughts and keeping them in our minds. It means stewarding every word, thought, impression, and revelation inspired by the Spirit of God.

The first half is taking captive every thought. One of the best ways to capture thoughts is a prayer journal. The second half is making it obedient to Christ — and that requires blood, sweat, and tears.

When I was nineteen years old, I heard a message about Benaiah, King David's bodyguard who chased a lion into a pit on a snowy day and killed it. When I listened to that message, a thought fired across my synapses: *If I ever write a book, I want to write one about that verse in the Bible.* I held captive that thought for nineteen years! Then I made it obedient to Christ by setting my alarm very early in the morning, sitting down at my keyboard, and writing a book titled *In a Pit with a Lion on a Snowy Day.* That book started out as a God-idea, but writing it was an act of obedience.

Nolan Bushnell, the creator of the Atari video game system, once stated, "Everyone who's ever taken a shower has had an idea. It's the person who gets out of the shower, dries off, and does something about it who makes a difference."

*Never underestimate the power
of a single prayer.*

Crazy Faith

"This woman is driving me crazy."
LUKE 18:5 NLT

I love the parable of the persistent widow. I don't mean any disrespect, but I think *persistent* is a nice word for *crazy*. This woman is crazy, but when the cause is a righteous one, it's a holy crazy!

We aren't told what injustice took place, but she was on a mission. Maybe her son was falsely imprisoned for a crime he didn't commit. Maybe the man who molested her daughter was still on the streets. We don't know for sure. But whatever it was, she wouldn't take no for an answer. And the judge knew it. The judge knew she would circle his house until the day she got justice or the day she died. The judge knew there was no quit in the crazy woman.

Does *the Judge* know that about you?

How desperate are you for the blessing, the breakthrough, the miracle? Desperate enough to pray through the night? How many times are you willing to circle the promise? Until the day you die? How long will you knock on the door of opportunity? Until your knuckles are raw? Until you knock the door down?

Like Honi the circle maker, the persistent widow's methodology was unorthodox. She could have, and technically should have, waited for her day in court. Going to the personal residence of the judge crossed a professional line. I'm almost surprised the judge didn't file a restraining order against her. But this reveals something about the nature of God. *God couldn't care less about protocol.* If He did, Jesus would have chosen the Pharisees as His disciples. But that isn't who Jesus honored.

Jesus honored the prostitute who crashed a party at a Pharisee's home to anoint His feet. Jesus honored the tax collector who climbed a tree in his three-piece suit just to get a glimpse of Him. Jesus honored the four friends who cut in line and cut a hole in someone's ceiling to help their friend. And in this parable, Jesus honored the crazy woman who drove a judge crazy because she wouldn't stop knocking.

The common denominator in each of these stories is crazy faith. People took desperate measures to get to God, and God honored them for it. Nothing has changed. God is still honoring spiritual desperadoes who crash parties and climb trees. God is still honoring those who defy protocol with their bold prayers. God is still honoring those who pray with audacity and tenacity. And the crazy woman is selected as the gold standard when it comes to praying hard. Her unrelenting persistence was the only difference between justice and injustice.

The viability of our prayers is not contingent on scrabbling the twenty-six letters of the English alphabet into the right combinations like *abracadabra*. God already knows the last punctuation mark before we pronounce the first syllable. The viability of our prayers has more to do with intensity than vocabulary. It has more to do with what we do than what we say.

Don't just pray about it; act on it.

There are defining moments in life when we need to prove to God that we mean business — and I don't mean "business as usual." In fact, it's only when "business as usual" goes out of business that we're in business — the Father's business. That's when we're on the verge of a spiritual breakthrough.

Crazy Is Normal

Josh Sexton pastors a church plant in North Carolina called Relevant Truth Church. God is doing amazing things at RTC. People who wouldn't darken the doorway of a church are finding a relationship with Jesus Christ at an indoor skate park that has been converted into a sanctuary. But like many church plants, there is more vision than money. RTC was facing the termination of their lease if they couldn't come up with the $3,500 rent when Josh got an idea while reading *The Circle Maker*. One of the leaders at RTC relayed what happened.

Josh asked me to come to the front during a worship service. He handed me a can of spray paint and asked me to paint a circle on stage. That's when Josh told us he wasn't going to leave the circle until God made provision for the church. With his wife's blessing, he brought in a bed and ordered a Port-a-John. All he had was his Bible and his prayer journal. Three times a day, his wife brings him meals. My wife and I live down the street, so we're helping with the kids.

I think Josh came to the place of desperation. If this thing was going to work, God was going to have to show up and show off. I really think he is planning on staying in that circle until God does something huge. Crazy huh?

Crazy?

Or maybe it's not crazy!

Maybe our normal is so subnormal that normal seems abnormal. Maybe we need a new normal. Bold prayers and big dreams are normal. Anything less is subnormal. And when bold prayers become the norm, so do the miraculous breakthroughs that follow.

I know there may be naysayers who find fault with Josh's approach, but sometimes you need to do something crazy, something risky, something dramatic. That's what Honi the circle maker did when he drew a circle in the sand and declared that he wouldn't come out until it rained. The San-hedrin almost excommunicated him because they thought his prayer was too bold. But you cannot argue with a miracle, can you? His radical prayer resulted in rain. And Honi was ultimately honored for "the prayer that saved a generation."

For the record, the Sanhedrin still exists in every organi-zation, every denomination, and every church. But don't let the nitpickers and naysayers keep you from doing something crazy if you know God has called you to do it. For the record, RTC didn't just get a new lease on their building; they got a new lease on their faith!

There is a pattern repeated in Scripture: crazy miracles are the offspring of crazy faith. Normal begets normal. Crazy begets crazy. If we want to see God do crazy miracles, sometimes we need to pray crazy prayers.

Bold prayers honor God and
God honors bold prayers.

First-Class Noticer

Devote yourselves to prayer,
being watchful and thankful.
COLOSSIANS 4:2

The word *watchful* is a throwback to the Old Testament – era practice of sitting on a city wall and keeping watch. Watchmen were the first ones to see attacking armies or traveling traders. They had the best vantage point. They saw things no one else saw. They saw things before others saw them. And this is precisely what happens when we pray. We see things no one else sees. We see things before others see them. We become God's watchmen.

Prayer is the difference between seeing with our physical eyes and seeing with our spiritual eyes. Prayer gives us a God's-eye view. It heightens our awareness and gives us a sixth sense that enables us to perceive spiritual realities that are beyond our five senses.

In their classic book *Geeks & Geezers*, business gurus Warren Bennis and Robert Thomas make an interesting observation about a common denominator among successful leaders in every field. Bennis and Thomas call them "first-class noticers."

Being a first-class noticer allows you to recognize talent, identify opportunities, and avoid pitfalls. Leaders who succeed again and again are geniuses at grasping context. This is one of those characteristics, like taste, that is difficult to break down into its component parts. But the ability to weigh a welter of factors, some as subtle as how very different groups of people will interpret a gesture, is one of the hallmarks of a true leader.

Prayer turns us into first-class noticers. It helps us see what God wants us to notice. The more you pray, the more you notice; the less you pray, the less you notice. It's as simple as that.

Let me explain how it works from a neurological perspective.

There is a cluster of nerve cells at the base of our brain stem called the reticular activating system that monitors our environment. We are constantly bombarded by countless stimuli vying for our attention, and it is the job of the RAS to determine what gets noticed and what goes unnoticed.

So you download a new ringtone. And you'd swear you've never heard it before, but after downloading it, it seems like everybody else has the same ringtone. It's not that lots of people went out and downloaded it when you did. It's the simple fact that when you downloaded that ringtone, it created a category in your RAS. That ringtone went unnoticed by you before you downloaded it because it wasn't important to you. Once you downloaded the ringtone, the RAS recognized it as relevant.

When you pray for someone or something, it creates a category in your reticular activating system. You start noticing anything related to those prayers. Have you ever noticed that when you pray, coincidences happen? And when you don't, they don't. It's more than coincidence; it's providence. Prayer creates divine opportunities. But prayer also sanctifies the reticular activating system and enables you to see the God-ordained opportunities that are all around you all the time. And once you see them, you have to seize them.

The Aramaic word for prayer *(slotha)* means "to set a trap." Opportunities are like wild animals. They are tough to capture. If you're going to seize them, you've got to set prayer traps.

We often think of prayer as nothing more than words spoken to God, but maybe it's more than that. Prayer is not a monologue; it's a dialogue. We speak to God with everything from words to groans to thoughts. And God speaks to us through dreams, desires, promptings, impressions, and ideas.

The Sixth Sense

There is an old adage: *Beauty is in the eye of the beholder.* In reality, *everything* is in the eye of the beholder. The emotions we experience don't reflect our external reality; they reflect our internal reality. We don't see the world as it is; we see the world as we are. That's why prayer is so critical. It's a way of seeing reality — and, more specifically, the reality that is beyond that reality we can perceive with our five senses.

Some things cannot be perceived with the five senses; they can only be conceived by the Holy Spirit. Some things cannot be deduced via deductive reasoning; they can only be imagined by the Holy Spirit. Some things cannot be learned by logic; they can only be revealed by the Holy Spirit.

The Holy Spirit compensates for our sensory limits by enabling us to conceive of things we cannot perceive with our five senses. Think of it as a sixth sense. The revelation of the Spirit gives us extrasensory perception, in the truest sense of that phrase. He helps us see the invisible and hear the inaudible. But that sixth sense has to be cultivated, much like our five senses do. Our spiritual vision develops much like our physical vision does.

When babies make their grand entrance into the world, their visual resolution is one-fortieth of that of a normal adult. They lack depth perception. And their visual range is only about thirteen inches. The world is low-definition, two-dimensional, and only thirteen inches in diameter. Slowly yet sovereignly, the world begins to take on width and breadth and depth. By four months, a baby can perceive stereoscopic depth. By six months, visual acuity has improved fivefold. Their black-and-white world has burst into a kaleidoscope of colors, and they have volitional control of their eye movements. And by his or her first birthday, the child sees the world almost as well as an adult.

Our spiritual eyes develop in much the same way. And prayer is the key to perception. Before our spiritual eyes are opened, the world is only thirteen inches in diameter. It's like living in a low-definition, two-dimensional world. Then the Holy Spirit gives us depth perception. He opens our eyes to see the ordinary miracles that surround us, the ordinary miracles that are us. It's like our spiritual cataracts are removed to reveal a reality that was always there. Like Jacob, we come to the ultimate realization: "Surely the LORD is in this place, and I was not aware of it."

When we open our spiritual eyes, we start seeing God everywhere we look. We see the image of God in others. We see His fingerprints on His creation. We see God-ordained opportunities all around us all the time.

It's something like what happens when we watch a film with 3D glasses; when we pray, God comes at us in ways that startle and thrill us.

We don't see the world as it is;
we see the world as we are.

Sow a Seed

*"If you have faith as small as
a mustard seed ..."*
MATTHEW 17:20

Standing beneath a giant sequoia is like standing in the shadow of the Creator. It was absolutely awe-inspiring on my first visit to Yosemite National Park. These magnificent creations can measure more than twenty feet wide and three hundred feet tall. The root system goes down about twelve feet and stretches out into an area about eighty feet in diameter. Their resistance to disease, insect damage, and fire make them almost indestructible. And their built-in ability to recycle and regenerate contributes to their two-thousand-year life span.

Now here is the amazing thing: the giant sequoia was once a seed. And that sequoia seed is no bigger than the seed that produces a tomato plant. That is the power of a single seed. And one sequoia, when it matures, will produce 400,000 seeds of its own every year. So in every seed, there isn't just a tree; there is a forest of trees.

Then God said, "Let the land sprout with vegetation — every sort of seed-bearing plant, and trees that grow seed-bearing fruit. These seeds will then produce the kinds of plants and trees from which they came."

And we just keep reading the Genesis account as if nothing happened. Granted, there are more spectacular creations than the simple seed — the sun, moon, and stars, for example. But the seed may be the most amazing example of God's prolific creativity. And we certainly owe God a thank-you for every kind of seed every time we bite into the fruit they produce — orange seeds, apple seeds, strawberry seeds, grapefruit seeds, pomegranate seeds, watermelon seeds.

Can you imagine life without any of these seeds?

William Jennings Bryan, famous for his role in the Scopes Monkey Trial in 1925, once likened the mystery of God to a watermelon seed:

I have observed the watermelon seed. It has the power of drawing from the ground and through itself 200,000 times its weight: and when you can tell me how it takes this material and out of it colors an outside surface beyond the imitation of art, and then forms in it a white rind and within that again a side of red heart, thickly inlaid with black seeds, each one of which in turn is capable of drawing through itself 200,000 times its weight — when you can explain to me the mystery of a watermelon, you can ask me to explain the mystery of God.

Mustard Seed

If we are going to understand the potential of faith, we have to understand the power of a seed. Jesus spoke of our faith in relation to a mustard seed, the smallest known garden seed in that culture. Like every seed, it needs to germinate, and this particular seed can take up to ten days to germinate. Some plants, like some dreams, take a lot longer. My dream of writing had to germinate for thirteen years! And some of my goals will take decades to accomplish! Faith is what keeps those dreams alive, even when it seems as though they are dead and buried. But that is the very nature of seeds. They go underground. They disappear. And while it may seem like they are dead, they are not. They're just germinating beneath the surface!

If you saw a mustard seed but didn't know what it was, you would have a hard time imagining what it could become. The potential is disguised in an awfully small package. You would have no clue that the mustard you put on your hot dog is the by-product of a tiny seed that was planted in the ground. You would have no idea what the seed would grow to become or how big it could get. And that is true of every seed. Would you guess that an acorn would become an oak? You'd never guess that a black seed would become a green watermelon with a red interior that tastes amazing!

In case you were wondering, the tiny mustard seed contains all the nutrients you need to survive. It's packed with vitamins B1, B6, C, E, and K. It's a source of calcium, iron, magnesium, phosphorus, potassium, selenium, and zinc.

Faith is a lot like that. It doesn't look like much, but we never know what it can become. A little faith goes a long way; in fact, a little faith will last an eternity.

The Speed of a Seed

Toward the end of his life, Honi the circle maker was walking down a dirt road when he saw a man planting a carob tree. Honi questioned him. "How long will it take this tree to bear fruit?" The man replied, "Seventy years." Honi said, "Are you quite sure you will live another seventy years to eat its fruit?" The man replied, "Perhaps not. However, when I was born into this world, I found many carob trees planted by my father and grandfather. Just as they planted trees for me, I am planting trees for my children and grandchildren so they will be able to eat the fruit of these trees."

This incident led to an insight that changed the way Honi prayed. In a moment of revelation, the circle maker realized that praying is planting. Each prayer is like a seed that gets planted in the ground. It disappears for a season, but it eventually bears fruit that blesses future generations. In fact, our prayers bear fruit forever.

Even when we die, our prayers don't. Each prayer takes on a life, an eternal life, of its own.

Because we are surrounded by technologies that make our lives faster and easier, we tend to think about spiritual realities in technological terms. We want to reap the very second we sow. We want God to microwave answers, MapQuest directions, and Twitter instructions. We want things to happen at the speed of light instead of the speed of a seed planted in the ground, but almost all spiritual realities in Scripture are described in agricultural terms. We want our dreams to become reality overnight. We want our prayers answered immediately. But that isn't the way it works in God's kingdom.

We need the patience of the planter.

We need the foresight of the farmer.

We need the mind-set of the sower.

We worry far too much about outcomes instead of focusing on inputs. We cannot make things grow. Period. All we can do is plant and water. But if we plant and water, God promises to give the increase.

This is both bad news and good news. We cannot break the law of sowing and reaping any more than we can break the law of gravity. No farmer would plant beans and expect to harvest corn!

If you sow kindness, you will reap kindness.

If you sow generosity, you will reap generosity.

If you sow love, you will reap love.

All of us go through times of spiritual, relational, or financial famines. It seems like the harvest will never come. And the temptation is to stop planting, but my advice is simple: sow a seed. Keep praying, keep obeying, keep giving, keep loving, keep serving. And if you keep sowing the right seeds, the harvest of blessing will come in God's time, in God's way!

If we do the little things like they are big things, then God will do the big things like they are little things.

One Day

One day
at about three in the afternoon
he had a vision.

ACTS 10:3

I love the two-word phrase in Acts 10:3: *one day*. It is pregnant with hope. Why? Because one day could be today. Today could be the day that God answers the prayer, performs the miracle, or keeps the promise!

In *one day*, God can deliver from an addiction that has held a person captive for years. In *one day*, God can bring back a prodigal child who has run away and been gone for decades. In *one day*, God can provide more than someone has accumulated in a lifetime. But if we are going to experience a miracle *one day*, we need to pray every day. Too many people pray like they are playing the lottery. Prayer is more like an investment account. Every deposit accumulates compound interest. And *one day*, if we keep making deposits every day, it will pay dividends beyond our wildest imagination.

$3 Million Miracle

One reason I love Acts 10:3 is because one of the greatest miracles I've ever experienced happened "one day at about three in the afternoon." I received a phone call on a Wednesday afternoon that changed the trajectory of my life personally and the life of our church corporately. Nothing could have prepared me to hear these words: "We want to give you three million dollars." I was absolutely speechless. And I'm a preacher! The caller graciously broke the awkward silence. He told me there were no strings attached and they wanted to remain anonymous. Then he explained the rationale behind the gift: "Pastor Mark, we love your vision and trust your leadership. There are some churches we wouldn't feel comfortable investing in because they wouldn't know what to do with the money, but you have vision beyond your resources."

That phrase will echo in my auditory cortex forever: *vision beyond your resources.*

That phrase has become a mantra at National Community Church and is inspiring us to continue dreaming irrational dreams. We certainly practice sound financial management, count the cost of every vision, and steward every penny in a way that honors God, but we refuse to let our budget determine our vision. That would be poor stewardship because it's based on our limited resources rather than on God's unlimited supply. Too often we butcher our God-given dreams because we forget the simple fact that God owns the cattle on a thousand hills. Don't let fear dictate your decisions. Letting your budget determine your vision is backward. Faith is letting your vision determine your budget. And if your vision is God-given, it will most definitely be *beyond your ability* and *beyond your resources*. Why? Because then God will get all of the glory! And I promise you this: *the God who gives the vision is the same God who makes provision.*

One Better

Our church is amazingly generous, but our median age is twenty-eight, which means most of our attendees are nowhere near their peak earning potential. They are faithfully tithing on their income as Hill staffers or inner-city schoolteachers or coffeehouse baristas, but they don't have the income or savings accounts to give large financial gifts. They are focused on paying off school loans or saving for a wedding. Over the course of thirteen years, the largest single gift we had ever received was a $42,000 tithe on the sale of a home. I honestly had no idea that anybody in our congregation had the means to give this kind of gift. I've since learned that the miracle is already in the house!

On March 15, 2006, we opened the doors to our coffeehouse on Capitol Hill. The total cost of building Ebenezer's Coffeehouse was about $3 million, and our mortgage was $2 million. One day, as I was praying, I felt prompted to pray for a $2 million miracle. The first thing I had to do was decipher whether this prompting was just my own desire to be debt-free or whether it was the Holy Spirit who dropped that promise into my heart. It's tough to discern between wishful thinking and prayerful promptings, but I was about 90 percent sure it was the Holy Spirit who put that promise in my heart. I had no idea how God would do it, but I knew I needed to circle that promise in prayer. I mentioned the $2 million miracle to four people in my prayer circle, and we started praying for God's provision.

Certainly weeks went by when I failed to even think or pray about the promise, but we did circle that $2 million promise off and on for four years. At one point, I got a little impatient and tried to manufacture the miracle with a start-up business. Unfortunately, what I thought was a $2 million idea turned into a $15,000 personal loss. I was tempted to give up when my plan failed, but we kept circling that promise in prayer. Then one day at about three in the afternoon, I got the phone call. The amazing thing is that we weren't even in a capital campaign. We weren't asking for money publically; we were just praying for it privately.

The moment I heard those words, "We want to give you three million dollars," I knew it was a fulfillment of the promise God had given us. I was, however, a little confused by the amount. We had been praying for $2 million, not $3 million. That's when the Holy Spirit seemed to say in a playful tone, *Mark, I just wanted you to know that I can do one better.* And, of course, He meant $1 million better!

Degree of Difficulty

Whenever I'm praying for something that is way beyond my ability or resources, I tend to pray longer and louder. I'll pull out the biggest theological words I know and pray in King James language. I mistakenly think my combination of words will somehow unlock the miracle, but I'm learning that God listens more to our hearts than our words. And what God loves more than anything else is childlike faith. It's our child-like faith, not our theological vocabulary, that moves the heart of our heavenly Father. It's simple childlike trust. It's the bedrock belief that God is bigger than our problem, bigger than our mistake, bigger than our dream.

When we pray, we tend to rank our requests by degree of difficulty. We see our requests as big or small, easy or difficult, simple or complex. But let me remind you of this simple yet profound truth: to the infinite, all finites are the same.

When Jesus walked out of the tomb, the word *impossible* was removed from our vocabulary. The size of your prayers depends on the size of your God. If your god is small, you'll pray man-sized prayers. But if your God knows no limits, then neither will your prayers. The God we pray to exists outside of the four space-time dimensions He created, and maybe we should pray that way!

I love the story about the man who sized up God in prayer one day. "God, how long is a million years to you?" God said, "A million years is like a second." Then the man asked, "How much is a million dollars to you?" God said, "A million dollars is like a penny." The man smiled and said, "Could you spare a penny?" God smiled back and said, "Sure, just wait a second."

A three million dollar gift was way beyond what I would have asked for or imagined, but then the miracle happened.

And even larger gifts have been given since that $3 million miracle. Please don't miss or dismiss what you're about to read: the way you steward the miracles of God is by believing for bigger and better miracles. God stretches your faith so you can dream bigger dreams.

Draw the Circle

God can accomplish more in one day than you can accomplish in a lifetime.

Speak to the Mountain

*"Say to this mountain,
'Move from here to there,'
and it will move."*

MATTHEW 17:20

There comes a moment when you must quit talking to God about the mountain in your life and start talking to the mountain about your God. You proclaim His power. You declare His sovereignty. You affirm His faithfulness. You stand on His Word. You cling to His promises.

Goliath held an entire army captive through fear. His weapon was intimidation. And that is how our enemy operates. He prowls around *like* a roaring lion. But the important word is *like*. He's an imposter. Jesus *is* the Lion of the tribe of Judah. And when He roars, everything is shaken. All authority under heaven and on earth is His. And we are His children. Why don't we live like it, love like it, give like it, serve like it, and pray like it?

If God is for us, who can be against us?
*The one who is in you is greater than the one who is in the
    world.*

I can do all things through Christ who strengthens me.
In all things God works for the good of those who love him,
who have been called according to his purpose.

What did Jesus do when Satan tempted Him in the wilderness? He fell back on the word of God. He used it like a skilled swordsman. And He wasn't just defending Himself; He was delivering blows by citing chapter and verse!

Maybe we need to quit playing defense and start playing offense. Maybe we need to quit letting our circumstances get between us and God and let God get between us and our circumstances. Maybe we need to stop talking to God about our problem and start talking to our problem about God.

More Than Conquerors

It's time to claim the victory that has already been won at Calvary. We are *not* conquerors; we are *more than conquerors* through Christ.

Jesus proclaimed the victory when He said, "I will build My church, and the gates of Hades shall not prevail against it." Let me make two observations. First, notice the pronouns. He did not say, "*You* will build My church"; He said, "*I* will build *My* church." The key pronouns are *I* and *My*. The church belongs to Jesus Christ. So does the battle. So does the victory.

Second, it says that the gates of Hades will not prevail. Gates are defensive measures, which means, by definition, that the church is on the offense. It's high time for an all-out attack on the enemy! The battlefield is the prayer closet. And secret prayer is our secret weapon.

When we hit our knees, we pick a fight with the enemy. We are immediately transported to the front lines of the kingdom, where we wage war with principalities and powers. That is where the battle is won or lost — on our knees! And when we hit our knees, God fights our battles for us.

Praying for Pharaoh

When we purchased the crack house that we turned into our coffeehouse on Capitol Hill, it took two miracles. The first miracle was getting the property; the second was getting it rezoned from residential to commercial.

For eighteen months, we met with everybody from the Historic Preservation Office to the Office of Planning to the Capitol Hill Restoration Society. We had overwhelming community backing. After all, we were investing $3 million to turn a crack house into a coffeehouse. But during the rezoning process, some influential neighbors decided to oppose our rezoning efforts because of misinformation about what we planned to do. I followed a link to a website where they were slandering our motives. To be honest, I was so upset I was ready for a throwdown! Their opposition had the potential to short-circuit our dream of building a coffeehouse, and I got angrier every time I thought about it. That's when I discovered the power of praying circles around the pharaohs in your life. And for the record, there will always be pharaohs who get in the way of what God wants to do in your life.

All of us have impossible people in our lives. All we can do is circle them in prayer. It's the only way to keep our attitude in check. And prayer has the power to change the heart of Pharaoh. So every time I got angry, I converted it into a prayer. I think it's the closest I've ever come to praying without ceasing because I was angry all the time.

I prayed for those neighbors for several months leading up to our hearing before the zoning commission. I'll never forget the feeling as we walked into the hearing room and sat down at our tables on either side of the aisle. I had absolutely no animosity toward the people who were opposing us. I felt an unexplainable compassion for the people who opposed us, and I wasn't worried about what they said or did because I had circled them in prayer. I had also circled the zoning commissioners. Not only did we win unanimous approval from the zoning commission, which is a testament to God's favor, but one of our opponents is now a regular customer at our coffeehouse!

The two-year ordeal of rezoning was emotionally and spiritually exhausting, but that is how to increase spiritual endurance. When it was all over, I thanked God for the opposition we encountered because it galvanized our resolve and unified our church. I learned that we don't have to be afraid of the enemy's attacks. These attacks are counterproductive when we counteract them with prayer. The more opposition we experience, the harder we have to pray. And the harder we have to pray, the more miracles God does.

*Quit talking to God about your problem
and start talking to your problem about God.*

Day 15

Contend for Me

Contend for me,
my God and Lord.
PSALM 35:23

God loves it when we fight for Him. But God loves it even more when we let Him fight for us! How do we do that? When we hit our knees, God extends His mighty right hand on our behalf. When we pray, He fights our battles for us. So keep fighting the good fight, but let God fight for you.

Prayer is the way we let go and let God. Prayer is the way we take our hands off and let God put His hands on. Prayer is the difference between you fighting for God and God fighting for you.

> Contend, LORD, with those who contend with me;
> fight against those who fight against me …
> Awake, and rise to my defense!
> Contend for me, my God and Lord.

I love the Hebrew word translated "contend" in these verses. It's two-dimensional. It refers to both physical combat and verbal combat. So it runs the gamut from cage fighting to courtrooms.

In terms of physical combat, God is like the mother grizzly that protects her cubs. It is God's instinctive nature because we are the apple of His eye. If anyone messes with us, they are messing with our heavenly Father.

In terms of verbal combat, God is like the defense attorney that pleads our case, pleads our cause. When our backs are against the wall, God has our backs. When everything is on the line, God steps in. Satan is the accuser of the brethren, but he's no match for the Paraclete.

The New Testament depiction of this is a little more defined. We actually have two intercessors. The Holy Spirit is interceding for us with groans that cannot be uttered. Long before we woke up this morning and long after we go to sleep tonight, the Holy Spirit was and is circling us in prayer. And if that doesn't infuse us with holy confidence, I don't know what will. But it isn't just the Holy Spirit who is interceding for us; the Son of God is interceding for us as well. They are interceding for the will of God to be accomplished in our lives. We are double circled. They are circling us all the time with songs of deliverance.

I made a determination a few years ago that I wasn't going to defend myself against any and every criticism that comes my way. Life is too short, and the mission is too important. And I'm called to play offense, not defense. God is my defender. And I believe He is contending for me if my cause is just and my heart is right.

It's important for us to have people in our lives who can speak words of rebuke and exhortation. But they will typically be someone with whom we have a relationship. When discerning whether to respond to criticism, I try to discern the spirit of the person doing the criticizing. Is the purpose redemptive or vindictive? And I put the criticism through the filter of Scripture. If it passes through the filter, then I need to repent. If it doesn't, then I don't let it pierce my heart. And I let God defend and contend on my behalf.

There are some battlefields I'm willing to die on, but there are some I'm not willing to die on. I won't engage in the combat of criticism. It is sideways energy, and it doesn't have a redemptive purpose. I overlook the offense so I can keep playing offense.

The First Official Prayer

On September 7, 1774, the Continental Congress held its first official meeting at Carpenter's Hall in Philadelphia. Their first official act was prayer. And it wasn't some perfunctory prayer that was nothing more than protocol; it was a good old-fashioned prayer meeting. Our founding fathers prayed with fervency and intensity. Earwitnesses heard them interceding several blocks away. Eyewitnesses said Henry, Randolph, Rutledge, Lee, and Jay were doubled over as they bowed in reverence before God. John Adams later recounted that it "has had an excellent effect upon every body here." And not surprisingly, General George Washington ended up on his knees. These revolutionaries knew their cause was doomed to fail without divine intervention. They prayed like it depended on God because they knew it did.

The pastor who led them in prayer that morning was

Dr. Jacob Duche. The Scripture he turned to? Psalm 35. He prayed that just as the Lord contended for David, God would contend for their cause if it were a righteous one. Dr. Duche's prayer is more than just a piece of our history; it's a piece of our destiny.

> *O Lord, our heavenly Father, high and mighty King of kings and Lord of lords, who dost from thy throne behold all dwellers on the earth, and reignest with power supreme and uncontrolled over all the kingdoms, Empires, and Governments; look down in mercy, we beseech thee, on these our American states who have fled to Thee from the rod of the oppressor and thrown themselves on Thy gracious protection, desiring to be henceforth dependent only on Thee ...*
>
> *Be Thou present, O God of wisdom, and direct the councils of this honorable assembly ... Shower down on them and the millions they here represent, such temporal blessings as Thou seeist expedient for them in this world and crown them with everlasting glory in the world to come. All this we ask in the name and through the merits of Jesus Christ, Thy Son and our Savoir. Amen.*

Our prayers don't have expiration dates. That's why I believe this prayer is still being answered 238 years later. It is part of our prayer genealogy as Americans. This was a genesis prayer. It was the very first prayer uttered at the start of the revolution. It was a prayer for every American henceforth. And it is still being answered. There is no other explanation for the improbability of America. God contended for our cause.

That is our history. That is our destiny.

I'm certainly not suggesting that America is always right and never wrong. Like every nation's history, ours is dotted with grievous sins. But the only explanation for the blessings we've experienced is the favor of God.

If you are on God's side, then God is on your side.

God will fight for you as you fight for Him.

And you can live with holy confidence, knowing that when God is contending for your cause, your cause is destined to succeed. This doesn't mean there won't be setbacks and sacrifices along the way; it just means the war has already been won.

 *Prayer is the difference between you fighting for God and God fighting for you.*

Lord, Surprise Me

"The wind blows wherever it pleases."
JOHN 3:8

A few years ago, a rather routine staff meeting turned into a prayer meeting. All of our staff ended up on their knees. I ended up on my face on the floor. And I prayed a prayer that has been repeated hundreds of times since then. In fact, it has become a prayer mantra: *Lord, surprise us.*

In one respect, this feels like a dangerous prayer because we have to put our plans on the altar. We have to relinquish control. We have to trust God's timing. But that prayer was motivated by a genuine desire to see God do something unprecedented — something that superseded our plans, something that we could not take credit for or control. And God has answered this prayer a thousand times in a thousand ways!

One of the most dramatic surprises happened a few weeks after praying that prayer for the first time. Our family was vacationing at a friend's cabin at Lake Anna, about ninety miles south of Washington, D.C. On the first day we heard a knock on the door. It was a neighbor named Harry, who asked if he could see the cabin. He looked harmless enough, so I invited him in. Within five minutes Harry had offered to let us use his pontoon boat for the week. When we went to his cabin to get the keys, I noticed a book on his coffee table written by a former senator who attended our church. I had a hunch when I saw the book that he might know the senator's good friend and my mentor, Dick Foth. Sure enough, Harry knew Dick. So I told Harry I would send him a copy of a book I had dedicated to Dick titled *Wild Goose Chase*. The week after our vacation ended, I sent Harry a copy, and he liked it enough to recommend it to his friend Tom.

Nearly a year after meeting Harry, I got a call from Tom, a deacon at Glen Echo Baptist Church. He introduced himself and explained that GEBC was once a thriving witness in their community but had dwindled to a dozen members. Then he told me they wanted to consider giving their two properties, valued at approximately $2 million, to National Community Church. I couldn't have been more surprised if he'd said I'd won the lottery without even buying a ticket. And that's what it felt like.

What profoundly impacted me was the fact that GEBC was courageous enough to recognize that the church was dying and generous enough to give its building to another church. We were surprised and humbled beyond words. Then I remembered our prayer: *Lord, surprise us.*

Can I make an observation? And I mean this with all due respect. Baptist churches don't give their churches to non-Baptist churches. To the best of my knowledge, it's unprecedented. But God always has a holy surprise up His sovereign sleeve. And when we pray, God throws surprise parties!

Every miracle, every blessing, every divine appointment has a genealogy. If we trace them back, we'll find a genesis prayer that set in motion the sovereign act of God. Am I saying that God *cannot do it* without us? No, I'm not saying He cannot; I am simply saying He *will not*.

In His omniscience and omnipotence, God has determined there are some things He will only do in response to prayer. The Bible puts it bluntly: "You do not have because you do not ask God." *If we don't ask, God can't answer.* It's as simple as that. The greatest tragedy in life is the prayers that go unanswered because they go unasked. I don't pretend to understand where the sovereignty of God and free will of humans meet, but it motivates me to work like it depends on me and pray like it depends on God. And if we do these two things, God will keep surprising us.

God Knows Every Tom, Dick, and Harry

Our family has a handful of sayings that have been passed down from generation to generation. They are part of our family folklore. I'm not sure where this one originated, but I remember my grandma stating it more than once: *you can't never always sometimes tell.* That tongue twister is a mind bender, so here's the translation: *anything could happen!*

Now let me redeem this saying and give it a prayer twist. When you circle a promise in prayer, you can't never always sometimes tell. Anything could happen. You never know when or how or where God will answer it. Prayer adds an element of surprise to your life that is more fun than a surprise party or surprise gift or surprise romance. In fact, prayer turns life into a party, into a gift, into a romance.

God has surprised me so many times that I'm no longer surprised by His surprises. That doesn't mean I love them any less. I'm still in awe of the strange and mysterious ways in which God works, but I have come to expect the unexpected because God is predictably unpredictable. The only thing I can predict with absolute certainty is this: *the more you pray, the more you will experience holy surprises.*

I love the reference to wind in John 3. I can't think of a better description of the way the Holy Spirit works. He is uncontrollable, unpredictable — which can cause angst or excitement. The choice is ours. About the wind, Jesus states, "You cannot tell where it comes from or where it is going." So it is with the Holy Spirit, says Jesus. In other words, *you can't never always sometimes tell.* But one thing is certain: if we follow Jesus, our lives will be anything but boring.

When I think about the degree of probability of what happened, it's mind-boggling. I have no idea what prompted Harry to knock on our door that day. If he hadn't knocked, I would not have gone over to his cabin, seen a book on his coffee table, mentioned Dick Foth, or sent him a copy of *Wild Goose Chase*. And, of course, I didn't know Tom from Adam! But God knows every Tom, Dick, and Harry! And He can orchestrate divine appointments with anyone, anytime, anywhere.

Lord, surprise us!

God always has a holy surprise
up His sovereign sleeve.

Do Not Delay

*"O Lord, pay attention and act.
Delay not, for your own sake, O my God."*
DANIEL 9:19 ESV

During our forty-day prayer challenge at National Community Church, our prayer circles were interceding for healing, jobs, marriages, deliverance, and salvation. And we saw each of those miracles happen, but there were speed bumps along the way. Praying hard is not the path of least resistance; it's usually the path of most resistance because we engage in spiritual warfare. In fact, when we begin interceding for others, we better make sure that others are interceding for us. We need a prayer circle that provides a prayer covering.

Very rarely are our prayers answered as quickly or easily as we'd like. By definition, praying hard is hard because it's hard. But it's the prayers you pray when you feel like you want to quit praying that can bring the greatest breakthroughs.

One woman in our church decided to circle her husband, who was applying for a job with the United States Attorney's office. On day two of the prayer challenge, Kelly went in for a second interview, but he didn't get the job. It was a bitter disappointment, and that is when most of us quit praying. But Kelly's wife, Charmaigne, kept circling.

The first day of the forty-day prayer challenge, I was praying about Kelly's job application at the U.S. Attorney's office in Alexandria. I prayed, "God, do not delay," but not through Daniel's prayer. Though it was frustrating that Kelly didn't get the job, I continued praying. I prayed that God would sustain us for the entire prayer challenge.

On the last three days of the prayer challenge, I was encouraged to read the book of Daniel. The Circle Maker teaches about praying through the Bible so I decided to do it. I prayed Daniel's prayer in 9:19: "O Lord, hear; O Lord, forgive. O Lord, pay attention and act. Delay not, for your own sake, O my God, because your city and your people are called by your name."

On the last day of the prayer challenge, God prompted me to do a full-day fast, and I prayed again for Kelly's job. I prayed using Daniel's prayer with a faith that God would not delay His answers. Indeed, God did not delay. The next day, the day after the prayer challenge ended, I got a voice mail from my husband that he got a job offer from D.C. Superior Court to clerk for a judge beginning in September. I immediately fell on my knees next to our dining table and thanked God for the miracle He had given us! It was the best gift ever after my constant praying and fasting. And guess what happened next? Another job was offered to him this week that started immediately and ends when his new job starts! God gave us more than what we asked for! Not one job, but two!

Our most powerful prayers are hyperlinked to the promises of God. When we know we are praying the promises of God, we can pray with holy confidence. We don't have to second-guess ourselves, because we know that God's word does not return to Him empty. This doesn't mean we can claim the promises of God out of context. But our problem typically isn't overclaiming the promises of God; it's underclaiming them.

> *Every spiritual blessing is ours in Christ.*
> *No matter how many promises God has made, they are "Yes"*
>   *in Christ.*
> *No good thing will God withhold from those whose walk is*
>   *blameless.*

If we stand *on* God's word, God will stand *by* His word.

I recently got an e-mail from a couple who put this principle into practice in a rather ingenious way. They went to Home Depot and bought paver stones. They inscribed ten biblical promises on the stones with white paint and laid them in their patio, and they stand on those promises every day in prayer. "One day when we have children of our own," they wrote, "we hope to give them these stones as a reminder of what it means to pray and to stand on the promises of God."

ALAT

Until recently, I attached an ASAP to every prayer. I wanted God to answer *as soon as possible*. But this is no longer my agenda. I don't want easy or quick answers because I have a tendency to mishandle the blessings that come too easily or too quickly. I take the credit for them, or I take them for granted. So now I pray it will take long enough and be hard enough for God to receive all of the glory.

I'm not looking for the path of least resistance; I'm looking for the path of greatest glory. And that requires high-degree-of-difficulty prayers and lots of circling.

Very rarely does our first prayer request hit the bull's-eye of God's good, pleasing, and perfect will. Most prayer requests have to be refined. Even "the prayer that saved a generation" didn't hit the bull's-eye the first time. Honi refined his request twice: "Not for such rain have I prayed." He wasn't satisfied with a sprinkle or torrential downpour. It took three attempts to spell out exactly what he wanted: "rain of Your favor, blessing, and graciousness." Honi drew a circle in the sand. Then he drew a circle within a circle within a circle.

I'm not praying ASAP prayers; I'm praying ALAT prayers. *As long as it takes.* I'm going to get in my prayer circle, and I'm not coming out until God answers. This doesn't mean I'm forcing God's hand. After all, we can't force God to do anything! It just means I'm praying with confidence. I believe that God never overpromises or underdelivers. He always delivers on His promises, but He does it on His timeline!

Draw the Circle

God is never early. God is never late.
God is always right on time.

Keep Circling

"On the seventh day,
march around the city seven times."

JOSHUA 6:4

I have a friend who moved to Washington, D.C., in 1994 to fight for a noble cause on Capitol Hill. Tony was deeply concerned that innocent children were being introduced to pornography simply because adult channels were one click away from cartoon channels, so he authored legislation that would force the cable industry to fully scramble pornography channels. As Tony prepared to visit all 435 House offices and 100 Senate offices, he decided to circle the Capitol in prayer seven times. He even let out a Jericho shout after the seventh circle!

Tony knew he couldn't win this fight without prayer. He also knew that prayer is the difference between *us fighting for God* and *God fighting for us.*

After praying seven circles, Tony started knocking on doors and asking for an audience with every member of Congress. Some of the offices applauded his efforts, but Tony was repeatedly told his efforts were too little, too late. The telecommunications bill he was trying to amend had already gone to markup. Tony was told there was no way the chairman of the congressional committee would reopen the bill to include his amendment because he'd have to reopen it to everybody else's amendments. Tony walked out of the 220th congressional office depressed and defeated. He was ready to throw in the towel and give up the fight when he had a burning bush moment.

I was on the second floor of the Longworth Building. I went over to a window, sat on its cold marble sill, and hung my head in defeat. I said to myself, "Stop wasting your time and go home to San Diego." Never before, and never since, has God spoken to me so clearly. While I sat there looking down at the marble-tiled floor, totally dejected, these words were spoken to me as clear as a bell: "Who is doing this — you or Me?" I can't explain how I felt when I heard those words, but I straightened up and responded, "You are, Lord!" Instantly I was filled with more excitement than when I had first begun. At each of the following 215 offices, my presentations were given with renewed faith.

Tony made his last presentation at the Canon Congressional Building. His amendment still seemed like a lost cause, but it's not over till God says it's over. If your cause is ordained by God, then the battle belongs to the Lord. It's His victory to win, not yours.

I am not exaggerating when I tell you this. As my leg crossed the threshold as I exited the 435th office, my pager went off.

Chairman Dingle had just agreed to allow my amendment to be added to his telecommunications bill.

Sometimes God shows up; sometimes God shows off!

God's timing is impeccable isn't it? He's never late. He's never early. God is right on time all the time! Is it a coincidence that Tony's pager went off just as he exited the last office? I think not. I don't believe in coincidences; I believe in providence. I believe there is a God in heaven who directs our steps, who prepares good works in advance, who causes all things to work together for good, who fights our battles for us! And if you pray through, there will be a breakthrough!

Don't lose heart. Don't lose hope. Don't lose faith. Don't lose patience.

Maybe you've been interceding for a child who has walked away from the faith. Maybe you've been believing for reconciliation in your marriage. Maybe you've been waiting for a healing miracle, a financial miracle, or an opportunity miracle.

Keep asking. Keep seeking. Keep knocking.

God rarely does things how or when we expect Him to, and it leads us to question His strange and mysterious ways. I'm sure the Israelites questioned God's battle plan at Jericho. They would have preferred to storm the gates or scale the walls, but God told them to circle the city for seven days! It didn't make any sense. It had to feel like forever. But they kept circling!

Sometimes God will push us to our absolute limits — the limits of our faith, of our patience, of our gifts. That is how

God stretches our faith and builds our character. Remember when God told Abraham to sacrifice his son Isaac? When God intervened and provided a ram in the thicket? God's intervention didn't take place until Abraham had put Isaac on the altar, tied him down, and raised the knife. God pushed Abraham to the precipice of logic. He tested Abraham to see if Abraham trusted Him. Abraham passed the test and got a testimony!

There is a branch of history called counterfactual theory that asks "what if" questions. It imagines how history would have unfolded differently if certain things had or had not happened. Let me play counterfactual theorist with biblical history.

What if the Israelites had stopped circling Jericho on day six? For that matter, *what if* Elijah had quit praying for rain after his sixth request? Or *what if* Naaman had only dipped in the river six times? And while we're on the subject, *what if* Tony had quit his door-to-door campaign after the 220th office?

The answer is obvious: *the miracle would have been forfeited right before it happened.*

I don't know what you've been circling for the past forty days or forty weeks or forty years. I don't know if you've gotten a *yes*, a *no*, or a *not yet*. You've got to praise God if the answer is *yes* and trust Him if the answer is *no*. If the answer is *not yet*, you've got to keep circling. It's always too soon to give up! What other option do you have? To pray or not to pray. Those are the only options.

None of my dreams have happened quickly or easily. There was nothing glamorous or glorious about the early days of our church plant adventure. There were certainly moments when I felt like quitting, when I was tempted to think all of our efforts wouldn't make much difference. After all, our average attendance was twenty-five people — and those twenty-five people could have found a much better church to attend. But I was thinking in present-tense terms. When you quit circling, you don't just compromise the present. Every promise, every miracle, every blessing in your future is forfeited. If I had called it quits, I would have bailed not only on the twenty-five people I was pastoring at the time; I would have bailed on the thousands we're influencing now and the tens of thousands we'll influence in the future!

If the Israelites had stopped circling Jericho, they would have forfeited their first victory in the Promised Land. But there was much more at stake than that. They would have forfeited the Promised Land altogether. But they didn't stop. They kept circling. And if you keep circling, the walls *will* come down. If you pray through, the breakthrough is inevitable.

Go ahead. Keep circling!

*If you don't get out of the boat,
you'll never walk on water.*

Memorial Offerings

*"Your prayers and gifts to the poor
have come up as a memorial offering
before God."*

ACTS 10:4

My grandfather had a prayer ritual that involved kneeling next to his bed at night, taking out his hearing aid, and praying for his family. He couldn't hear himself without his hearing aid, but everyone else in the house could. Few things leave a more lasting impression than hearing someone intercede for you by name. These prayers are some of my earliest memories.

Grandpa Johnson died when I was six years old, but his prayers did not. Our prayers never die! When we pray, our prayers exit our four dimensions of space-time. Our prayers have no space or time limitations because the God who answers them exists outside of the four dimensions He created. You never know when His timeless answer will reenter the atmosphere of our lives, and that should fill us with holy anticipation. Never underestimate His ability to answer anytime, anyplace, anyhow. He has infinite answers to our finite prayers. He can answer them more than once. And He answers them forever.

Acts 10:4 declares that our prayers are memorial offerings. I cannot promise that God will answer your prayers *how you want* or *when you want*, but I can promise that God will answer. He always answers! At critical points in my life, the Spirit of God has whispered to my spirit: *Mark, the prayers of your grandfather are being answered in your life right now.* Those sacred moments rank as the most humbling and exhilarating moments of my life.

Like a parent who collects their children's elementary artwork and displays it prominently on a refrigerator door, the heavenly Father loves our prayers. Each one is a keepsake. Each one functions like a memorial that jogs the memory of the Almighty.

If our prayers are that precious to God, shouldn't they be more significant to us? Aren't they worth collecting like snapshots in a family photo album? Shouldn't they be treated with respect and dignity, like the monuments that grace the nation's capital?

Every prayer we utter is like the marble stones used in the building of the Washington Monument or Lincoln Memorial. When we pray, we are building a monument to God, a memorial to Him. And those prayers are not perishable. They aren't wood, hay, or straw. They are a foundation of gold, silver, and costly stones.

They will not be forgotten. They will not go unanswered.

Eternal Prayers

I recently met with a pastor-friend who is a circle maker. I've met very few people who pray with more intensity, more specificity, more consistency. Over lunch, Wayne told me a story about his grandmother, and it was evident that the apple didn't fall far from the tree. Intercession is part of their spiritual DNA as a family.

Wayne's grandmother raised twelve children while managing their household. After every meal she prepared, she would go to her bedroom to pray. Three times a day, the children could hear her interceding for them by name. When she was on her deathbed at the age of ninety-one, the entire family gathered at the family home. She invited them into the bedroom where she prayed three times daily. Then she prophetically declared to her twelve children, "I'm going to die, but the power of my prayers will come to pass in each of your lives."

Her predominant prayer was that every member of her family would surrender their lives to the lordship of Jesus Christ. At the time, six children were following Christ, and six weren't. That was fifteen years ago. The tally is now ten *yes* and two *no* — or maybe I should say in faith, *not yet*. Wayne shared with me how the tenth *yes* (the oldest child) came to Christ.

My grandmother's oldest son is named Johnny. A month ago, his next-door neighbor had a dream in the middle of the night about Johnny. The neighbor felt compelled to invite him to church, and he accepted the invitation that Sunday, which happened to be Palm Sunday. When he walked into that church, all he could hear was his mother's voice calling out his name in prayer. The pastor asked if anybody wanted to put their faith in Jesus, and Johnny raised his ninety-two-year-old hand. He got baptized the next weekend on Easter Sunday.

I did the math. Wayne's grandmother passed away when Johnny was seventy-seven years old. From the day he was born until the day she died, she prayed for him three times a day. If you add it up, that is 84,315 memorial offerings. She didn't get to see the answer to her prayers on this side of the space-time continuum, but she will be one of the first people to greet her son when he steps into eternity!

Did her prayers have anything to do with the neighbor's middle-of-the-night dream? I cannot imagine they were unrelated. And that is the beauty of prayer. We never know when our prayers will be answered, and we never know when we are the answer to someone else's prayer. You might be the answer to 84,315 prayers! When we live by faith, we will harvest prayer seeds that have been planted for decades, for centuries, for millennia. When we live by faith, those memorial offerings turn into crowns of glory. Prayer offerings turn into praise offerings.

Our prayers don't die when we do.
God answers them forever.

Go. Set. Ready.

He [Abraham] did not know where he was going.

HEBREWS 11:8

You'll never be ready.

You'll never be ready to get married. You'll never be ready to have kids. You'll never be ready to start a business or go back to school or move to the mission field. You'll never be ready financially, emotionally, or spiritually. You'll never have enough faith, enough cash, or enough courage. And if you are looking for an excuse, you will always find one.

I never have been, and I'm sure I never will be, ready for anything God has called me to do. This doesn't mean I haven't prepared myself. I've worked hard getting an education, but I've come to terms with the fact that I'll never be ready for anything God has called me to. And that's OK. God doesn't call the qualified; He qualifies the called.

If you wait until you're ready, you'll be waiting for the rest of your life.

The author of Hebrews writes, "By faith Abraham, when called to go to a place he would later receive as his inheritance, obeyed and went, even though he did not know where he was going" (11:8).

Abraham didn't know the final destination, but it didn't keep him from taking the first step in the journey. What's the first step or next step you need to take in your journey? If you take the first step, God will reveal the second step. The problem is that most of us want the twenty-five-year plan before we're willing to step out in faith. We want to know exactly where we're going and exactly when we'll get there, but God doesn't operate that way. He gives us just enough revelation, just enough grace, just enough strength. Why? So we will live in daily dependence on Him. He doesn't want us to rely on the revelation; He wants us to rely on Him.

Without knowing where he was going, Abraham took the first step. And God honored it. There are moments in life when you need to quit a job, make a move, or end a dating relationship. And you need to take that step without knowing what the next step will be. Don't wait for more revelation; be obedient to the amount of revelation God has given you.

Why Not?

There is an old adage: *ready, set, go*. And I know it's predicated on the importance of preparation. But I think it's backward. You'll never be ready. You'll never be set. Sometimes you just need to go for it. The sequence of faith is this: Go. Set. Ready.

Some people spend their entire lives getting ready for what God wants them to do, but they never end up doing it because they never come to the realization that they'll never be ready. This is where so many of us get stuck. Our failure to act on what we know God is calling us to do not only breeds doubt and discouragement; it's a form of disobedience.

Nearly two thousand years ago, Jesus said "Go." So why do we operate with this red-light mentality? Why are we waiting for the green light we've already been given?

The vision of National Community Church is to have twenty locations by the year 2020. Launching new locations is part of our DNA. But when we launched our first multisite location, there was a little resistance to the idea. Some people asked why. And on one level, this is a fair question. But I honestly think it's the wrong question. The real question is, "Why not?"

Why wouldn't we continue to launch new locations and try to reach more people? Why wouldn't we continue to do more of what God is blessing? Why wouldn't we multiply?

As Christ-followers, we are called to take a *why not* approach to life. It's an approach to life that dares to dream. It's an approach that's bent toward action. And it doesn't look for excuses not to do something. Don't get me wrong. It's awfully difficult to discern the will of God. Even after prayer and fasting, it usually entails making tough decisions. And I'm certainly not advocating a thoughtless or prayerless approach to decision making. We need to know that God is calling us to devote our lives to missions, take the internship offer, quit our job, or make the move. But I wonder if we're so afraid of doing the wrong thing that it keeps us from doing the right thing.

Get Off the Ship

My friend Dr. George Wood has an amazing painting in his office of an African man standing on a high hillside overlooking the ocean. There is a large steamship on the horizon and a smaller canoe coming toward the shoreline. In this instance, the story is worth a thousand paintings. It symbolizes the importance of going before we're set or ready.

In 1908, newly commissioned missionaries John and Jessie Perkins were on board a steamship rounding the coast of Liberia. They knew God had called them to Africa, but like Abraham, they didn't know exactly where God wanted them to go. So they purchased tickets and trusted that God would tell them where to get off. As the ship made its way around Garraway Point, they sensed the Holy Spirit was prompting them to get off the ship.

Unknown to the Perkinses, there was a young man living in the region named Jasper Toe. He was a God-fearing man who practiced the religious rituals passed down by his ancestors, but he had never heard the name of Jesus. One night he looked into the night sky and prayed a simple prayer: "If there is a God in heaven, help me find You."

As Jasper stood under the stars, a voice he had never heard before spoke to him. "Go to Garraway beach. You will see a box on the water with smoke coming out of it. And from that box on the water will come some people in a small box. These people in this small box will tell you how to find Me."

Jasper Toe traveled seven days on foot to Garraway beach, arriving on Christmas Day, 1908. From the shore he saw a black box — a steamship — floating on the water with smoke coming out of it. And that is when John Perkins and his wife sensed the Holy Spirit saying, "Get off the ship here. This is where I want you to go."

When they went to the captain of the ship and asked him to let them get off the ship, he said, "I can't let you off the boat here. This is cannibal country. People go in there and never come back."

John Perkins insisted, "God wants us to get off the boat."

The captain brought the steamship to a halt, and the Perkinses were placed in a mammy chair that swung them over the side of the ship. They got into a canoe along with all of their belongings, and they rowed to shore in that little box. When they got to the shore, Jasper Toe was waiting to welcome them. He motioned for them to follow him, and they did. They could not speak each other's language, but the Perkinses followed Jasper Toe all the way back to his village. They eventually learned the language of the people there. They started the first church in that village. And Jasper Toe was their first convert.

Those who knew Jasper Toe described him as one of the godliest men they had ever met. And his legacy is the hundreds of churches he helped to establish in the country of Liberia.

What if the Perkinses had ignored the prompting of the Holy Spirit? What if they had dismissed that God-idea as a bad idea? What if they had asked *why* instead of *why not*? What if they had decided to play it safe and stay on the ship?

I'm sure God could have intervened in another way. And

I would like to think He would have. But who can calculate the opportunity costs when we ignore the promptings of the Spirit, thereby missing divine appointments? Faith is not faith until it is acted on.

Go. Set. Ready.

Draw the **Circle**

If you are looking for excuses,
you will always find one.

Set Your Foot

*"I'm giving you every square inch
of the land you set your foot on."*
JOSHUA 1:3 MSG

Since the release of *The Circle Maker*, I've received a steady stream of e-mails and letters from readers who have started circling their dreams, homes, and workplaces in prayer. An inner-city teacher circles her classroom; a real estate agent prays circles around the properties she represents as a listing agent; a team of doctors and nurses have turned their patient rounds into prayer circles. A member of Congress is circling the Capitol, and an NFL chaplain is circling his team's practice facility. One reader even circled his bank, praying for a financial miracle — until law enforcement intervened. They thought he was casing the joint!

There is nothing magical about physically circling something in prayer, but there is something biblical about it. The Israelites circled the city of Jericho until the wall came down. That's what a forty-day prayer challenge is all about. Too often we quit circling almost as soon as we start. Drawing prayer circles is a metaphor that simply means "praying until God answers." It's a determination to pray as long as it takes, even if it takes longer than you ever imagined.

Drawing prayer circles isn't some magic trick to get what you want from God. God is not a genie in a bottle, and your wish is not His command. His command better be your wish. If it's not, you won't be drawing prayer circles; you'll end up walking in circles.

Drawing prayer circles starts with discerning what God wants, what God wills. And until His sovereign will becomes your sanctified wish, your prayer life will be unplugged from its power supply. And getting what you want isn't the goal; the goal is glorifying God by drawing circles around the promises, miracles, and dreams He wants for you.

Pray a Perimeter

Over the years, I've drawn prayer circles around promises in Scripture and promises the Holy Spirit has conceived in my spirit. I've drawn prayer circles around impossible situations and impossible people. I've drawn prayer circles around everything from life goals to pieces of property. But let me go back to my first prayer circle and retrace my steps.

When I was a twenty-two-year-old seminary student, I tried to plant a church on the north shore of Chicago, but that plant never took root. Six months later, fresh off a failed church plant, Lora and I moved from Chicago to Washington, D.C. The opportunity to attempt another church plant presented itself, and my knee-jerk reaction was to say no, but God gave me the courage to face my fears, swallow my pride, and try again.

There was nothing easy about our first year of church planting. Our total church income was $2,000 a month, and $1,600 of that went to rent the D.C. public school cafetorium where we held Sunday services. On a good Sunday, twenty-five people showed up. That's when I learned to close my eyes in worship because it was too depressing to open them. I felt underqualified and overwhelmed, which put me right where God wanted me. It is how we learn to live in raw dependence, and raw dependence is the raw material out of which God performs His greatest miracles.

One day as I was dreaming about the church God wanted to establish on Capitol Hill, I felt prompted by the Holy Spirit to do a prayer walk. I often paced and prayed in the spare bedroom in our house that doubled as the church office, but this prompting was different. I was reading through the book of Joshua at the time, and one of the promises jumped off the page and into my spirit:

> "I'm giving you every square inch of the land you set your foot on — just as I promised Moses."

As I read this promise given to Joshua, I felt that God wanted me to stake claim to the land He had called us to and pray a perimeter all the way around Capitol Hill. I had a Honi-like confidence that just as this promise had been transferred from Moses to Joshua, God would transfer the promise to me if I had enough faith to circle it. So one hot and humid August morning, I drew my first prayer circle. It still ranks as the longest prayer walk I've ever done and the biggest prayer circle I've ever drawn.

Starting at the front door of our row house on Capitol Hill, I walked east on F Street and turned south on 8th Street. I crossed East Capitol, the street that bisects the NE and SE quadrants of the city, and turned west on M Street SE. I then completed the circle, which was actually more of a square, by heading north on South Capitol Street. I paused to pray in front of the Capitol for a few minutes. Then I completed the 4.7-mile circle by taking a right turn at Union Station and heading home.

The prayer circle had taken nearly three hours to complete because my prayer pace is slower than my normal pace, but God has been answering that three-hour prayer for the past fifteen years. Since the day I drew that prayer circle around Capitol Hill, National Community Church has grown into one church with seven locations around the metro D.C. area. And all of the properties we own — Ebenezer's Coffeehouse, our theater on Barracks Row, and an $8 million piece of property that we own debt free — are right on that circle.

Coincidence?

More like providence!

When the Israelites circled Jericho, they had no idea how God would give them the city. But they didn't let what they didn't know keep them from obeying the command they had been given. So they circled the promise over and over and over again. They circled the promise thirteen times over seven days! Why? Because even though they didn't know *how* God would deliver on the promise, they knew that God would come though somehow, someway!

And God didn't just show up; God showed off His power. He toppled the wall of Jericho like it was a game of Jenga!

God is not a genie in a bottle,
and your wish is not His command.
His command better be your wish.

Prayer Fleece

"I will place a wool fleece on the threshing floor."
JUDGES 6:37

Anna is a twenty-three-year-old professional dancer from England whose life was turned upside down after reading *Wild Goose Chase* three years ago. Anna now runs a dance studio in Serbia that ministers to the poorest of the poor, but let me tell you how she got there.

Psalm 37:4 states that when you take delight in the Lord, God will give you the desires of your heart. The word *give* means "to conceive." As you press into God's presence, old sinful desires die, and new holy desires are birthed in your spirit. These single-cell desires ultimately become lifelong dreams if we nurture them in prayer.

Anna was living her dream, making a living by doing the very thing she loved most. Then she got a distinct impression one day that she needed to use her dancing for God. She wasn't sure what it meant, but she couldn't shake it. It kept her company during the day and kept her awake at night. Her friends assured Anna that she was making a difference right where she was, but she knew there was something else, something more. Then one day she read about a ministry project in Serbia, and something came alive in her spirit. She felt she needed to go visit, but she didn't know the first thing about Serbia. In fact, she had never met a Serbian. That's when Anna put a prayer fleece before the Lord: *Lord, if You want me to visit this ministry in Serbia, then let me meet a Serbian this week.*

Anna shared her prayer fleece with her friends, and even though they thought it was a crazy prayer, they agreed to circle it with her. Two days later, a tall, dark-haired gentleman walked into the dance studio where Anna was practicing. Anna was sure he was Italian, but she went ahead and asked him where he was from. When he told her he was from Serbia, she said, "You're the one I've been waiting for."

Six months later, Anna packed a suitcase and her guitar, bought a one-way ticket, and moved to Serbia. She works with the lowest-income Serbians, teaching English, the Bible, and dance to the children. Anna has gone from performing on stage for the *Who's Who* of Great Britain to choreographing dance performances for children with disabilities. And she's loving every second of it. But it started with a prayer fleece.

Her next God-idea? To open an Ebenezer's-styled coffeehouse in Serbia. That's why she sent me a letter. Actually, she called it a *prayer letter*. I think it was another fleece of sorts. I was so impacted by Anna's prayer letter that I shared her story, and Anna's dream made its way into the hearts of others. A handful of people stepped up and said they wanted to be shareholders in that ministry. And with the exchange rate, a few American dollars can turn into quite a few Serbian dinar.

Caution

There are moments when we need to turn our desires, ideas, and dreams into prayer fleeces. Now, we have to be very careful when it comes to putting fleeces before the Lord. Generally speaking, signs don't precede our steps of faith; signs follow. But there are occasions when it's OK to ask God for confirmation because of our uncertainty. I don't think we should do it often, and we shouldn't approach it in a haphazard manner that amounts to nothing more than picking petals off a daisy, saying, "She loves me; she loves me not."

So here are a few cautions when it comes to fleeces. First, if God has already answered your question in Scripture, then you don't need to even ask it. Don't seek revelation when God has already given it. Second, check your motives to make sure they aren't selfish. The fleece must come out of a genuine desire to honor God and do His will. Third, you have to be willing to accept whatever answer you receive without second-guessing it.

When God called Gideon to become a judge in Israel, he was filled with insecurity. When the angel addressed him as "mighty warrior," I bet Gideon looked over his own shoulder to see who he was talking to because there was no way it could be him! He thought God was making a mistake. "How can I rescue Israel? My clan is the weakest in the whole tribe of Manasseh, and I am the least in my entire family!"

But I love God's answer: "I will be with you."

That's all we need to know, isn't it? If we could come to grips with two fundamental truths, they would transform our lives: *God is with us*, and *God is for us*. That is all you ever need to know. God is with you, and God is for you. Let it sink into your spirit. And as Romans 8:31 states, "If God is for us, who can be against us?"

The angelic encounter wasn't enough for Gideon. He needed more confirmation, so he devised a test. He put a fleece before the Lord not once but twice. And God patiently reassured Gideon because Gideon asked out of genuine humility.

> "If you are truly going to help me, show me a sign to prove that it is really the LORD speaking to me."

In 2003, when National Community Church was preparing to become a multisite church and launch our second location, I was filled with uncertainties and insecurities. We were venturing into uncharted territory without a map. During an all-day prayer and planning meeting, we concluded we wanted to launch in the movie theaters at Ballston Common Mall in Arlington, Virginia. We closed our daylong meeting asking God for favor and a sign, a prayer similar to the one that Gideon prayed. We had been negotiating with Regal Cinema for three months but had kept hitting a wall. They only wanted to give us early morning access, and the additional time was cost prohibitive. After months of getting nowhere in negotiations, and the day after we put a prayer fleece before the Lord, Regal changed its corporate pricing structure. It's safe to say that in the world of leasing, if you want more time, you pay more money. And if you mysteriously get more time for less money, it has to be a sign from the Lord. It was just the sign we needed, and it catapulted us into one church with two locations.

Ask God

One of my prayer heroes is George Müller. Along with pastoring one church for sixty-six years, he established the Ashley Down orphanage. Müller cared for 10,024 orphans while establishing 117 schools for their education throughout England. In today's dollars, George Müller raised somewhere in the neighborhood of 150 million dollars. That is an amazing feat, but what makes it even more amazing is that he never asked anyone for a penny. He felt compelled to only ask God when he had a need. He trusted that God knew exactly what he needed, so he turned every need into a prayer. When he needed a pipe fixed, he prayed for a plumber. When he needed food or money or books, he prayed that God would provide. It is estimated that more than 30,000 specific prayers recorded in his journals were answered. And just for the record, the most impressive and most important statistic may be this one: Müller read the Bible cover to cover more than 200 times!

Müller prayed like it depended on God, but he also worked like it depended on him. Müller wrote, "This ... is one of the great secrets in connection with successful service for the Lord; to work, as if everything depended upon our diligence, and yet not to rest in the least upon our exertions, but upon the blessing of the Lord." The key to kingdom productivity is this: work really hard at what God has called you to do, but do not trust in your work; trust in God.

Oswald Chambers once wrote, "Let God be as original with other people as He is with you." This piece of advice has become a personal mantra. *Be yourself.* So I'm not prescribing George Müller's approach to prayer for everyone. It was a personal covenant he felt led to make with God. But we can learn from his example. Maybe we've been asking the wrong person — a boss, spouse, friend, or colleague. Maybe we need to ask God.

Don't seek answers; seek God. And the answers will seek you.

Draw the Circle

When God gives a vision,
He always makes provision.

Not Now

"Wait for the gift my Father promised."
ACTS 1:4

When God says no to a prayer, it doesn't always mean *no*; sometimes it means *not yet*. It's the right request but the wrong time.

A few years ago, Lora and I were house hunting on Capitol Hill. We had lived on the Hill since 1996 when we were fortunate enough to buy a hundred-year-old row home during a buyers' market. As our kids got bigger, our fifteen-foot-wide row home seemed to get smaller, so we started looking for a little larger place. We discovered our dream home less than a block away, and we decided to make an offer, but we also knew our financial limits. After praying about it, we came up with our best offer and felt like it was a fleece. If God wanted us to have the house, the owner would accept our offer. With the real estate market lagging and the time on market increasing, we were confident the seller would accept our offer. He did not. And as much as we wanted the house and as tempted as we were to go beyond our predetermined offer, we walked away. We had already done the interior decorating in our imaginations, so we were definitely disappointed. But we also had complete peace because we had prayed about it.

We stopped looking at homes for a year. Then one night, as we drove by the house we had tried to purchase, Lora said, "Do you ever feel like that is the house that got away?" We had driven by the house a hundred times, and Lora had never said a thing. But her casual comment must have been a subconscious prayer because the next morning a For Sale sign went up in the yard. That's when I had a holy hunch that God's *no* a year earlier was really a *not yet* and was about to turn into a divine *yes*.

What Lora and I didn't know is that the owner had never sold the house! It sat on the market for 252 days with no buyer and then was taken off the market. When the same owner put the house back on the market, we decided to make the *same offer*. It was a calculated risk because he'd already said no once, but it was another prayer fleece. We told our real estate agent it was our final offer. We were willing to walk away a second time, but this time the owner accepted the offer — and God answered our prayer one year after we thought He would. What we thought was a *no* was actually a *not yet* that turned into a *yes*!

Sometimes we have to be willing to give something up *to God* in order to get it back *from God*. Like Abraham's willingness to sacrifice Isaac, it will probably be something that is precious to us. It may even be a gift from God, just like Isaac was to Abraham. But God will test us to make sure the gift isn't more important than the Gift Giver, the dream isn't more important to us than the Dream Giver. He'll test us to make sure it's not an idol. If it is, that dream, gift, or desire might need to die so that it can be resurrected. But God often takes things away to give them back so that we know they are gifts to be stewarded for His glory.

Going through a death and resurrection makes us appreciate our house more than we would have otherwise. And the beautiful thing isn't that *we own the house*; it's that *the house doesn't own us*. When something is given back after it is taken away, whether it's a house or our health, we don't take it for granted.

Now here's the icing on the cake. By waiting a year to buy the house, our house actually went up in value by 10 percent because the real estate market in D.C. had rebounded. So we got our dream house for the same amount of money and sold our old house for a lot more money than we would have a year earlier! It was definitely worth the wait. And tithing on the sale of our house was one of the easiest checks we've ever written because God's hand of blessing was so evident.

Wait

I hate to wait. I don't like waiting at red lights. I don't like waiting at the doctor's office. I don't like waiting in drive-throughs for fast food. It's never fast enough. I don't even like waiting for December 25, so we start opening gifts on Christmas Eve!

You name it, I don't want to wait for it. But waiting is part of praying, and praying is a form of waiting. Prayer will sanctify our waiting, so we wait with holy expectancy. And waiting doesn't delay God's plans and purposes. It always expedites them. Waiting is the fast track to whatever it is that God wants to do in our lives. And we'll discover that on God's timeline, a day is like a thousand years, and a thousand years are like a day.

In our impatience, we often try to do God's job for Him. We treat Sabbath observance like a luxury instead of a commandment. We only obey it when it's convenient, and then we discover that it's never convenient. We work as though the world revolves around us and relies on us. Maybe it's time to rest as though the world revolves around and relies on the Creator who hangs the stars and spins the planets.

Let me come right out and say it: we're way too busy. In the words of the apostle Paul, we're "busybodies." We're constantly trying to do more and more in less and less time. The net result is that we don't have any margins in our lives. And that is when prayer gets marginalized. We think we have too much to do to pray, but the exact opposite is true: we have too much to do *not* to pray! Martin Luther once declared, "I have so much to do that I shall spend the first three hours in prayer." The more you have to do, the more you have to pray!

After the ascension of Jesus, the disciples didn't immediately "go into all the world." Why? Because Jesus left explicit instructions: "Do not leave Jerusalem, but wait for the gift my Father promised." Instead of immediately embarking on their mission, they waited in Jerusalem for the Holy Spirit. They didn't try to get ahead of God. They gathered in an upper room and prayed for ten days. Those ten days have been paying dividends for two thousand years.

After we pray like it depends on God, we need to work like it depends on us. But if we don't pray first, our work won't work. We can't do something for God until we let God do something for us. He wants to fill us with His Holy Spirit, but we need to empty ourselves first. From the depths of our hearts to the depths of our minds, the Holy Spirit wants to fill every crevice that already exists and create new capacities within us. And when the Holy Spirit comes on us, we will think new thoughts and feel new feelings. It's part of the package deal.

But you have to wait for it.

The question is this: How long are you willing to wait?

What would happen if we holed up in an upper room, knelt at an altar, or locked ourselves in a prayer closet and said, "I'm not coming out until I receive the gift my Father promised." I'll tell you exactly what would happen: Pentecost would happen all over again.

You cannot plan Pentecost. It's not like Peter woke up on the day of Pentecost and had "speaking in tongues" on his to-do list. He didn't plan on baptizing three thousand people that day. But if you pray for ten days, Pentecost is bound to happen.

 Draw the Circle

Sometimes God's no simply means not yet.

Find Your Voice

The word of the LORD came to me.

JEREMIAH 1:4

When I was nineteen years old, the Holy Spirit awakened me from my sleep in the middle of the night. It had never happened before, and it has never happened since. I grabbed my Bible and knelt at the foot of my bed. When I flipped the Bible open, it landed on Jeremiah 1. I started reading it, and it started reading me. In the original context, God was speaking to Jeremiah, but it was as though the Holy Spirit was speaking directly to me. Jeremiah's calling is my calling.

I didn't fully understand the ramifications or implications of this singular event that took place more than two decades ago. In fact, I still don't. God's callings aren't understood or accomplished in months or years or decades. It usually takes a lifetime. And one verse in particular always confused me.

> "Before I formed you in the womb I knew you,
>   before you were born I set you apart;
>   I appointed you as a prophet to the nations."

It's the last sentence that didn't make sense: "I appointed you ... to the nations."

It confused me because I've never felt called to be a missionary. I didn't know how that part of the calling would be fulfilled. That's when a friend sent me an e-mail that opened my eyes and helped me connect the dots.

I'm speaking at a national leadership conference for the nation of Malaysia and visited the largest bookstore in Kuala Lumpur today. I was thrilled to see your book in a very visible place in the religious section. I stopped to praise God for the influence He has given you to the nations!

It was the last phrase that caught my attention: *to the nations.*

I feel as called to write as I do to pastor, but I never viewed my writing as being *prophetic* or *international.* Then it dawned on me that my books are translated into more than a dozen languages. In a moment of revelation, I realized that God had fulfilled His promise, and I didn't even know it. I was appointed to the nations, but not by moving to a mission field. My books are like messages in a bottle that land on distant shores.

I've received countless letters from readers all around the world, but I never connected the dots. I just didn't know that God would fulfill this part of my calling in this particular way. But that's how God works, isn't it? He tricks us. We think we're going somewhere to do something, but God always has ulterior motives. There is a rhyme and reason to His will that we aren't even aware of.

Voiceprint

All of us have a unique voiceprint, not just physically but spiritually as well. God wants to speak through you differently than through anyone else. Your life is a unique translation of Scripture. It doesn't matter what you do — politician, preacher, entertainer, homemaker, teacher, musician, lawyer, or doctor. You are called to be a prophetic voice to the people God places in your life. But the key to discovering your prophetic voice is cultivating a prophetic ear. If you want to find your voice, you need to hear the voice of God.

During a recent trip to Ethiopia, I met several amazing leaders. A group of about a dozen political, medical, and business leaders meet regularly as part of a Bible study. God is using them to shape a country and a continent. I met a woman who plays a pivotal role in the African Union, a doctor who is building a hospital in a rural region of Ethiopia, and a developer who is designing the first PGA-quality golf course of its kind in East Africa. What I discovered during my visit is that they have one thing in common: all of them spend one day a week in prayer and fasting. Many of them don't even go into work on that day! We may be tempted to think they're less productive because they give up a day of work, but maybe they are more productive because they waste far less time on nonproductive pursuits.

We live in a culture in which everybody wants to be heard, but many people have nothing to say. Don't worry about building a platform. If you listen to God, people will listen to you. Why? Because you'll have something to say! And God will give you a platform to speak from.

So how do we hear the voice of God?

The first thing to do is open your Bible. When you open your Bible, God opens His mouth. The surest way to get a word from the Lord is by getting into God's Word. God will speak *to* you. Then God will speak *through* you.

In the process, make sure you have no unconfessed sin in your life. Sin doesn't just harden the heart; it also hardens our hearing. In fact, it makes us turn a deaf ear to God because we don't want to hear the convicting voice of the Holy Spirit. But if you aren't willing to listen to the convicting voice of the Spirit, you won't hear His comforting voice, forgiving voice, or merciful voice either. Sin creates relational distance, and distance makes it harder to hear the still, small voice of the Holy Spirit. But if you get close to God, you won't miss a thing He says. And if you incline your ear to God, God will incline His ear to you.

When too much white noise invades my life and I'm having a hard time hearing the voice of God, I'll often go into a season of fasting. Fasting is like noise cancellation. It helps me tune out the voices I shouldn't be listening to and tune into His frequency. It's still difficult to distinguish between our own thoughts and the inaudible voice of the Holy Spirit, but just like a relationship with a loved one, we begin to discern His voice more accurately. Eventually, it'll be like the voice of a spouse or child. We'll be able to interpret even the subtlest intonations.

If you want to find your voice,
you need to hear the voice of God.

A Prophetic Voice

"I wish that all the LORD's people were prophets."
NUMBERS 11:29

During the 2012 NCAA basketball tournament, I heard a postgame interview with Buzz Williams, coach of the Marquette Screaming Eagles. Following a victory that advanced their team to the Sweet Sixteen, Coach Williams referred to his players as "lion chasers." That caught my attention because I use this phrase repeatedly in my book *In a Pit with a Lion on a Snowy Day*. It turns out that his pastor, who went to college with me, gave Buzz a copy of the book. He and many of his players read it right before March Madness began.

During the off-season, Buzz flew out to D.C. so we could spend a few hours together. We discovered that pastors have something to learn from coaches, and coaches have something to learn from pastors. Buzz is the first person to admit he's a "work in progress." So am I. But I love the fact that his intensity for Jesus matches his intensity for basketball. And he's not just interested in how his kids perform on the court; he's investing in them for eternity.

Only four of the kids on Buzz's current squad know their biological father. Only two of them come from a family with an intact marriage. Many of the kids on his team didn't have a father's voice of love or discipline, so Buzz is that voice.

During the first one hundred days of a freshman's involvement in his program, Buzz meets with them on a daily basis. They come to his office, and he prays with them, even the kids who don't believe in God. Buzz told me he's had a few awkward silences! After praying with each other, they embrace each other. And Coach Williams tells them he loves them.

I think Buzz sees his squad of twelve the way Jesus saw His twelve disciples. And isn't that how we should see every person whom God has intentionally put in our lives — family members, friends, colleagues, and neighbors? Buzz is more than a coach who sees athletic potential in his players; he is a prophet who sees the spiritual potential. And he knows that those two things are not unrelated.

Personal Prophecies

Prayer isn't just the way we cultivate our own potential; prayer is the way we recognize potential in others. Like Paul, who saw gifts in Timothy that Timothy couldn't see in himself, we, through prayer, are enabled to see with prophetic eyes. We are given supernatural insight. Then we are prepared to speak with prophetic boldness into the lives God has positioned in our path.

Jewish philosophers did not believe that the prophetic gift was reserved for a few select individuals; they believed that becoming prophetic was the crowning point of mental and spiritual development. The more we grow in grace, the more prophetic we become.

This doesn't mean we will start predicting the future; it means we'll start creating it. How? Through our prayers! Prayer is the way we write the future. It's the difference between letting things happen and making things happen. And when we speak prophetic words into someone's life, it gives them a new lease on life.

According to 1 Corinthians 14:3, a prophet speaks words of comfort and encouragement as prompted by the Holy Spirit. And prophets come in all sizes and shapes. But the common denominator is prophetic insight that is the by-product of intercessory prayer. The more we pray, the more prophetic we will become. And I know it's a play on words, but the less we pray, the more pathetic we will become. Sorry, I couldn't resist, because it's true.

Laurie Beth Jones has stated that at least 40 percent of our lives are based on personal prophecies. I'm not sure how to substantiate this statistic, but I find it very believable. The right word spoken at the right time can make an eternal difference. In *The Power of Positive Prophecy*, Jones gives a great example of how one prophetic word can change a person's destiny:

> I grew up in an alcoholic household where I never heard a positive word. On my way home from school I would always stop in at Jimmy's, the local dry cleaner, because he kept candy on the counter. He got to know me, and told me one afternoon, "Michael, you are a very smart

boy. Someday you are going to run a very big business." I would listen to him in disbelief and return home only to get called a "dog" and knocked around by my dad. But you know … Jimmy the dry cleaner was the only person I can remember believing in me … Today I run a multimillion-dollar health care organization, just like Jimmy predicted. I guess you could say that a dry cleaner was the prophet in my life.

You may not see yourself as a prophet, but you are one. You're a prophet to your friends. As I write about in *Praying Circles around Your Children*, parents are prophets to their children. You're a prophet at work and a prophet at home. And your words have the potential to change lives by helping people discover their identity and destiny in Jesus Christ.

Sometimes you need the courage to rebuke. When you catch kids doing something wrong, for example, lovingly remind them of this: *that's not who you are*. And when you catch them doing something right, reinforce it. Celebrate what you want to see more of. That's one way to fan into flame the gift of God.

You don't have to influence thousands of lives to make a difference. Maybe you're called to influence one person who will influence thousands. You sow into their life so they can reap a harvest. The fruit of their life is your reward.

I've always been inspired by something that the former Secretary-General of the United Nations Dag Hammarskjöld said: "It is more noble to give yourself completely to one individual than to labor diligently for the salvation of the masses."

At critical junctures in my life, God has sent prophets across my path. They were ordinary people — a missionary named Chris Smith, a college professor named Opel Reddin, a mentor named Dick Foth. God used them to speak the right word at the right time. God gets all the glory for everything He does in us and through us, but there are people along the way who get some credit as well.

Prayer is the way we recognize potential in others.

Game with Minutes

Pray without ceasing.

1 THESSALONIANS 5:17 NASB

On January 30, 1930, Frank Laubach began a prayer experiment he called "the game with minutes." He was dissatisfied with his lack of intimacy with God and decided to do something about it. One of the inspirations for Laubach's experiment was Brother Lawrence, a seventeenth-century monk whose singular purpose in life was to live in the presence of God. For Brother Lawrence, this didn't mean retreating from the routine of life; it meant redeeming every routine and turning it into a prayer. For decades, Brother Lawrence worked in the kitchen of his Carmelite Monastery, washing dishes and preparing meals, but he turned his chores into prayers. After many years of practicing the presence of God, prayer became a way of life. In the words of Brother Lawrence, "The time of business does not with me differ from the time of prayer; and in the noise and clatter of my kitchen, while several persons are at the same time calling for different things, I possess God in as great tranquility as if I were upon my knees at the blessed sacrament."

Inspired by the example set by Brother Lawrence, Laubach embarked on his prayer experiment. The driving motivation was a question that consumed every waking moment: *Can we have contact with God all the time?* His life became a quest to answer that question. Like an explorer embarking on a voyage of discovery, Laubach set sail on his prayer experiment. He chose to make the rest of his life an experiment in answering that question.

Laubach described "the game with minutes" in these terms:

> We try to call Him to mind at least one second of each minute. We do not need to forget other things nor stop our work, but we invite Him to share everything we do or say or think. Hundreds of us have experimented until we have found ways to let Him share every minute of our waking hours.

One of the ways that Laubach played this game was shooting people with silent prayer. He didn't cock his thumb, use his index finger to fire, and then blow away the imaginary smoke; he simply prayed for people while looking at them. Some people would walk by without any reaction, but others would do a sudden about-face and smile at him. Sometimes a person's entire demeanor would change. The simple act of praying for everybody he encountered turned the routine of life into a daily adventure.

I discourage using an actual shooting motion, but what a great way to pull the trigger on 1 Timothy 2:1: "I urge, then, first of all, that petitions, prayers, intercession and thanksgiving be made for all people." Putting this passage into practice is as simple as praying for people before or after meeting with them. Before walking into a meeting, pray for the people you are meeting with. Ask God for favor, discernment, and grace. Then when you leave, pray a blessing on them. A prayer of blessing isn't just something for pastors to pronounce over congregations at the end of services. If you are a child of God, you are a priest. It's your right and responsibility to pronounce blessings over everyone in your life — from your children to your colleagues to your customers, and everyone in between.

Prayer Routines

The key to praying without ceasing is turning everything into a prayer. It usually starts with the big things like problems and dreams. Then it graduates to little things like chores and routines. And eventually, your entire life becomes a continuous prayer.

Every thought. Every action. Every moment.

If you are a worrier by nature, I have good news for you. You have tremendous prayer potential. The apostle Paul writes, "Don't worry about anything; instead, pray about everything." If you worry about everything, you'll have a much higher likelihood of praying without ceasing if you simply learn to turn your worries into prayers. The Holy Spirit can redeem your anxious thoughts by using them as prayer triggers. Think of worry as a prayer alarm. Every time it goes off, you put it to prayer. And when you do, you'll discover that your anxieties will evaporate like early morning fog. So quit wasting your worries. Redeem them by recycling them. Turn your worries into prayers!

What if you stopped reading the newspaper and started praying it? What if you turned lunch meetings into prayer meetings? What if you turned your chores into prayers?

You'd come a lot closer to the goal of praying without ceasing!

When you are folding your children's laundry, pray that they would be clothed with the righteousness of Christ. When you're commuting to and from work, cast your cares on Him. When you tuck your kids into bed at night, let the last words they hear be your prayers for them.

One of my newest and most meaningful prayer routines is kneeling by my bed at the beginning of every day. It's the first thing I do. I climb out of bed and get on my knees. I want God to have my first thoughts, my first words.

It dials me into God's frequency. It sets the tone. It postures me for the entire day.

Holy Experiment

Six months into his game with minutes, Laubach wrote about his holy experiment in his prayer journal.

Last Monday was the most completely successful day of my life to date, so far as giving my day in complete and continuous surrender to God is concerned ... I remember how as I looked at people with a love God gave, they looked back and acted as though they wanted to go with me. I felt then that for a day I saw a little of that marvelous pull that Jesus had as He walked along the road day after day "God-intoxicated" and radiant with the endless communion of His soul with God.

The reason most people don't feel intimacy with God is that they don't have a daily prayer rhythm. They may have a weekly rhythm of going to church, which is wonderful, but doing so in and of itself won't produce intimacy with God. Can you imagine talking with your spouse or child once a week? God wants a day-by-day, hour-by-hour, minute-by-minute relationship with you.

The good news is this: God is only a prayer away. The shortest distance between you and God is the distance between your knees and the floor. But you don't have to hit your knees or bow your head or fold your hands to be heard. Prayer isn't something we do with our eyes closed; prayer is something we do with our eyes wide open. Prayer isn't a sentence that begins with "Dear Jesus" and ends with "Amen." In fact, the best prayers don't even involve words at all. The best prayer is a well-lived life, day in and day out.

Turn your prayer life into a game. Try experimenting with a new posture like walking or kneeling. Try experimenting with different types of fasts — from food to television to sleep to Facebook — but remember that the key is giving something up and replacing it with prayer. Try praying at different times, like first thing in the morning or last thing at night. Try experimenting with different techniques. Create a prayer list or begin journaling your prayers.

If you want God to do something new in your life, you cannot keep doing the same old thing. My advice is simple: do something different. And you'll see what a difference it makes!

Draw the Circle

Change of pace + Change of place = $\dfrac{Change\ of}{perspective}$

Double Circle

"This kind goeth not out but by prayer and fasting."
MATTHEW 17:21 KJV

For thirteen years I was a frustrated writer. I had a half-dozen half-finished manuscripts on my computer, but I couldn't seem to finish a book. I started to think that the dream of writing a book might be nothing more than a mirage. Finally, when my level of frustration hit an all-time high, I decided to do a forty-day media fast out of desperation. That fast was the turning point in my writing career. I needed a breakthrough, but it took more than prayer; it took prayer plus fasting. In the process, I found that my writing became a form of praying. I don't type on a keyboard; I pray on it. And by the time I was done, I had completed my first self-published book.

There are times when circling something in prayer isn't enough. We need to double-circle it with prayer and fasting. Matthew 17:21 tells us that certain miracles only happen in response to prayer and fasting. In the same way we open a double combination lock, we need to both pray and fast to unlock the miracle. And the combination of these spiritual disciplines doesn't just add up; it multiplies their effectiveness. Fasting will take us further into the presence of God than praying, and it will get us there much faster. We still need patience and endurance, but fasting has a way of fast-tracking our prayer life like a hyperbolic chamber that speeds healing or a hyperlink that gets us someplace with one click. Fasting is hyperprayer.

There are many different kinds of fasts. I do a twenty-one-day Daniel fast at the beginning of every year that consists of just fruits and vegetables. I sometimes fast from sunrise to sundown. And I occasionally do a complete food fast for short periods of time. But while the most obvious kind of fast involves food, a media fast can be just as powerful. If we want to hear the voice of God, we've got to get rid of the white noise in our lives. A television fast or Facebook fast may be precisely what we need to hear God's voice more clearly.

No matter what we fast, we need to establish a time frame and an objective. If we don't determine exactly when the fast starts and finishes, we'll find excuses to compromise and probably quit. So we must establish a start date and an end date and then figure out what we're fasting for.

We can fast for deliverance from the yoke of bondage. We can fast for the discernment to make a decision. We can fast for favor. We can fast to dedicate something to God — a new year, new job, or new business. We can fast for a financial, relational, or emotional breakthrough. Or we can fast simply to seek the heart of God.

The Flesh

On the eve of his crucifixion, Jesus was in Gethsemane praying hard. His disciples were supposed to be praying, but they were sleeping instead. You can hear the disappointment in Jesus' voice when He asked them, "Couldn't you men keep watch with me for one hour?"

That challenge is worth circling. Take it literally. Take it personally.

I'm convinced that one hour of prayer will revolutionize our lives in ways we can't even begin to imagine. It will help us tap into new dimensions of God's power. It will help us reach out in love, even to the most difficult people. And it will give us the wisdom we need to navigate our greatest challenges.

The disciples let Jesus down when He needed them most. Their failure didn't just hurt Jesus; Jesus knew that it would hurt them. Let me play counterfactual theorist with a question: Would Peter have disowned Jesus if he had been praying instead of sleeping? Maybe he let Jesus down because he wasn't prayed up? While I can't prove it, I think Peter would have passed the temptation test if he had prayed through. His betrayal started when he fell asleep in the garden instead of praying through. That is where the battle is won or lost.

Then Jesus gets to the heart of the matter: "The spirit is willing, but the flesh is weak."

Truer words were never spoken.

Most people have a willing spirit. It's the weak flesh that gets in the way. The problem isn't desire; the problem is power and, more specifically, willpower. That's where fasting comes into play. The reason fasting gives us more power to pray is because it's an exercise in willpower. Physical discipline gives us the spiritual discipline to pray through.

To be honest, I struggle with fasting more than any other spiritual discipline for one simple reason: I love food. But fasting is the way I say to God, *I crave You more than I crave food.* I've also found that saying no to food helps me say no to whatever my flesh craves. It's like a spiritual workout that strengthens my willpower. If I can say no to food, I can say no to other forms of temptation.

When we work out, we break down our muscle fibers so they can be built back up even stronger. In much the same way, fasting breaks down our pride, our bondages, our will. It helps us break bad habits and build good habits. Fasting is the way we break down our spiritual calluses and regain sensitivity to the Holy Spirit.

And if we will live in a place of brokenness, God will build us back up in the power of the Holy Spirit. After forty days of fasting, Jesus' body was undoubtedly in a weakened state. But Scripture states, "Jesus returned to Galilee in the power of the Spirit."

Empty Stomach

I'm more and more convinced that the answer to every prayer is more of the Holy Spirit. Need more power? Then you need more of the Holy Spirit. Need more wisdom? Then you need more of the Holy Spirit. Need more love, joy, peace, patience, kindness, goodness, faithfulness, gentleness, or self-control? Then you need more of the Holy Spirit.

We need to be filled with the Holy Spirit, but we have to empty ourselves first. And one of the best ways to empty ourselves is through fasting.

When I have a big decision to make, I circle it with a fast. It doesn't just purge my body; it purges my mind and spirit as well. It also purges my motives. When I need a breakthrough, I circle it with a fast. It doesn't just break down the challenges I'm facing; it also breaks down the calluses in my heart.

An empty stomach may be the most powerful prayer posture in Scripture. It's even more powerful than kneeling! It shows God that we mean business. And when we fast, God makes our business His business!

Maybe there is something you've been praying for that you need to start fasting for. You need to take it to the next level. Draw a double circle by fasting for a friend or a family member. During our forty-day prayer challenge, small groups turned into prayer circles by fasting for friends who were battling cancer or applying for jobs or fighting to save marriages. And the answers were absolutely amazing. If you double-circle things with prayer and fasting, don't be surprised if you receive a double blessing!

If you want to break the sin habit, you've got to establish a prayer habit.

Quit Praying

"Well done, good and faithful servant!"
MATTHEW 25:23

One of the defining moments in my prayer life happened a decade ago. I was in a small group with a friend who worked for InterVarsity Christian Fellowship at Georgetown University. Jeremy was working on a shoestring budget, and their campus ministry needed a computer. He shared the request at the end of our meeting, and I agreed to pray for it, but when I started praying for it, I felt that the Lord wanted me to stop praying. It was like the Holy Spirit said, "Why are you asking Me? You're the one with the extra computer!" I quit praying in midsentence. I told Jeremy we didn't need to pray about it because I had an extra computer he could have.

I wonder how many of our prayer requests are within our own power to answer? Yet we ask God to do what we can do ourselves. And then we wonder why God doesn't respond. Maybe it's because God won't do for us what we can do for ourselves. God isn't honored by prayers that are within the realm of human possibility; God is honored when we ask Him to do what is humanly impossible. That way, God gets all the glory!

There are some things we don't need to pray about. We don't need to pray about loving our neighbors. We don't need to pray about giving generously or serving sacrificially. We don't need to pray about blessing someone when it is in our power to do so. We don't have to pray about turning the other cheek or going the extra mile. God has already spoken on those subjects.

There comes a moment when praying becomes a form of spiritual procrastination. It's time to stop praying and start acting.

Quit praying about the program and fill out an application. Quit praying for the friend you hurt and make a phone call. Don't just complain to God about your coworker; circle them in prayer. Don't just pray for missionaries; write a check.

One of my heroes is Peter Marshall, the former chaplain of the United States Senate. His prayers at the opening of Senate sessions are timeless. Peter Marshall believed in an action-oriented approach to Scripture.

> I wonder what would happen if we all agreed to read one of the Gospels, until we came to a place that told us to do something, then went out to do it, and only after we had done it ... began reading again? ...
>
> There are aspects of the Gospel that are puzzling and difficult to understand. But our problems are not centered around the things we don't understand, but rather in the things we do understand, the things we could not possibly misunderstand.
>
> This, after all, is but an illustration of the fact that

our problem is not so much that we don't know what we should do.

We know perfectly well ... but we don't want to do it.

Please don't misinterpret what I'm saying. Pray about everything. Then pray some more. But at some point, we have to quit praying and start acting. One of the great mistakes we make is asking God to do for us what God wants us to do for Him. We confuse roles. For example, we try to convict those around us of sin. But that is the Holy Spirit's responsibility, not ours. In the same sense, God won't do for us what we can do ourselves. And many of us get stuck spiritually right there.

We are called to pray about everything, but there comes a time when praying can be a form of disobedience, laziness, or negligence. We can't just pray like it depends on God; we also must work like it depends on us.

Action Verb

When Christianity turns into a noun, it becomes a turnoff. Christianity was always intended to be a verb — more specifically, an action verb. The title of the book of Acts says it all, doesn't it? It's not the book of *Ideas* or *Words*. It's the book of *Acts*. And if we said less and did more, I believe we would have the same kind of impact the first-century church had. And while we're on the subject, we should be more known for what we're *for* than what we're *against*.

Prayer that doesn't lead to action isn't true prayer; it's self-talk. When we talk to God, God will talk back to us. He will provoke us, rouse us, stir us, goad us, and prompt us. When we say "amen," inaction is no longer an option.

I'm always challenged by members of our congregation who leave everything they know to go to a mission field in another part of the world. They are the true heroes of the kingdom. A few years ago, Becky pursued her God-ordained passion halfway around the world to a little village in India. Why? Because she couldn't just pray about the injustice she had witnessed; she had to do something about it.

I went to India to work with women and children who were trafficked into sex slavery. Most of these women were Nepalese and ended up working as forced prostitutes in India's infamous red-light districts. Their children were literally born into brothels and knew nothing of life except violence, rape, and hunger. Although I wasn't able to rescue the women from their situation, I was able to offer hope and empowerment for the survivors and children. I led dance therapy sessions, helping to reconnect the survivors to their bodies and allowing them to see themselves as beautiful creations of God.

The area we were working in was devastatingly poor and malaria infested. And as an antitrafficking activist, I was in danger from the traffickers and brothel owners. My parents pleaded with me to leave, but I couldn't stay away. I could see God in each of their bloodshot, traumatized, beautiful eyes, begging me to touch, to comfort, to hug, and ultimately to love them.

If Christians believe that the image of God is in every person, why don't we act like it? Why do we turn our eyes from the poor, the widows, the orphans, and the prostitutes? Although prayer is necessary and helps bring comfort, it's not enough to truly alleviate suffering. God didn't send His Son to pray for us but rather to act for us. The only thing that upsets me more than downright evil acts are people who allow injustice to happen with their inaction. Jesus transformed God's message into action, and it should be our mission to devote our lives to similar action.

When everything is said and done, God won't say, "Well said, good and faithful servant." He won't say, "Well thought," "well planned," or even "well prayed." There is only one commendation He will give: "Well done, good and faithful servant."

Don't just pray about it; do something about it.

A New Prayer

Sing to the LORD a new song.
PSALM 96:1

Spiritual growth is a conundrum. The key to spiritual growth is developing healthy and holy routines called spiritual disciplines. But once the routine becomes routine, we need to change the routine. Why? Because sacred routines become empty rituals if we do them out of left-brain memory instead of right-brain imagination.

Routines are a necessary and important part of life. Most of us practice a morning ritual that includes showering, brushing teeth, and putting on deodorant. On behalf of family and friends, please continue practicing those routines. But here's the catch-22: good routines become bad routines if we don't change the routine. One of the great dangers we face spiritually is learning how and forgetting why. Call it familiarization. Call it habituation. Call it routinization. Call it whatever you want, but when we learn how and forget why, we start going through the motions spiritually.

A few years ago, I came across a fascinating study indicating that we stop thinking about the lyrics of songs after singing them thirty times. I'm sure the numbers vary a bit from person to person, but the tendency is universal. And it has profound implications when it comes to worship. If we aren't careful, we aren't really worshiping God; we're just lip-synching. In fact, the lyrics can get in the way of genuinely expressing to God our own thoughts, our own feelings.

Can you imagine a marriage in which the only expression of love is through Hallmark cards? You never put your love into your own words; you just use someone else's words. That's how many of us worship God. We never go beyond the lyrics that someone else has written. Without lyrics on a screen, we'd have nothing to say, nothing to sing.

Six times the psalmist tells us to sing a new song. Evidently God gets tired of old songs. He doesn't want you to worship Him with just your memory; He wants you to worship Him with your imagination as well. Love isn't repetitive; love is creative. As love grows, you need new lyrics and new melodies. You need a new song to express new dimensions of love. If you express your love to your wife in the same way over and over again, she may stop believing you at some point. Why? Because it's a mindless expression of an old feeling.

Right-Brain Prayer

Left-brain worship doesn't cut it. Neither does left-brain prayer.

Jesus warns us, "When you pray, don't babble on and on as people of other religions do. They think their prayers are answered merely by repeating their words again and again.

Don't be like them, for your Father knows exactly what you need even before you ask him!"

It's easy to fall into a prayer rut. We repeat all the prayer clichés we know, followed by an amen! In the same way that we need to sing a new song, we need to pray a new prayer. We need a new vocabulary, a new methodology.

We tend to think and act in patterned ways. Our tendency to do things the way we've always done them is called a heuristic bias. It is an amazingly complex cognitive process, but the result is mindlessness. We do things without thinking about them. If we aren't careful, we pray without thinking — and that is just as destructive as thinking without praying.

A few years ago, I preached about overcoming our heuristic bias, and someone in our congregation was compelled to respond with a prayer experiment.

After your sermon, I decided to approach your challenge to thank God for the daily miracles we generally take for granted. Knowing the list of thanks could be infinitely long, I decided to focus only on the miracles I was receiving at the moment of my prayer. So I started praying. "Thank You, God, for aerobic respiration. Thank You for mitochondria, which right now are creating ATP. Thank You for ATP. Thank You for glycolysis. Thank You for pyruvate."

With a biology degree, I ended up having a lot of things on the list. By the time I got back to my place in Arlington, I was thanking God for each of the amino acids. "Thank You, God, for glycine. Thank You for leucine and isoleucine and tryptophan."

I started thanking God for the fact that all organisms that form amino acids have the same chirality so that my body can reuse the nutrients and cellular building blocks of the food I break down. I found myself in absolute awe of His creation.

I prayed while I took a walk outside, thanking Him for bones and ligaments and tendons. I also thanked Him that I somehow never took an anatomy course in college, because otherwise I would have felt compelled to thank Him for each bone by name, which would have definitely set me back even more in my quest to get through most of the miracles I was receiving at that moment.

I spent the day praying without ceasing! I literally didn't stop and just consciously kept listing things I was thankful for. I listened to music and thanked Him for my ear's cochlea. While I made dinner, I thanked Him for xylem in the plants I was preparing. I spent a lot of time thanking Him for the molecular properties of water. I thanked Him for the bacteria in my colon that helps me digest food. I thanked Him for the genetic recombination that made developing and cultivating cotton plants possible for the jeans I was wearing.

At around nine o'clock that night, I think God got amused with the futility of me trying to thank Him for everything. The Spirit finally hushed me, saying, "You can stop now."

Now that's a right-brain prayer!

God doesn't want all of us to pray the same way. We pray in keeping with our personality. So one dimension of my own prayer life is humor. We burst out laughing in the middle of prayer all the time because I'll bust out a joke. I know that sounds sacrilegious, but I love telling jokes. Why would I exclude God? And I can't imagine a relationship with someone where humor wasn't part of our conversational relationship. It would be downright boring. I'm not sure God laughs at all my jokes, but He's the one who created us with a sense of humor.

The next time you pray, try a new posture or a new time slot. If you typically verbalize your prayers, try writing them out. If you kneel while praying, try a prayer walk. Do something different. Get out of your regular routine, and pray a new prayer to the Lord.

 *If you want God to do something new, you cannot keep doing the same old thing.*

Abide in Me

"If My words abide in you ..."
JOHN 15:7 NASB

In ancient Jewish culture, formal education began at six years of age. Jewish boys enrolled in their local synagogue school called *bet sefer* ("house of the book"). On the first day of class, according to tradition, the rabbi would cover their slate with honey. Honey was the symbol of God's favor. Then the rabbi would instruct his students to lick the honey off their slate while reciting from Psalm 119: "How sweet are Your words to my taste! Yes, sweeter than honey to my mouth." It was their first lesson and their most important lesson. It taught the students that nothing is sweeter than the Word of God. It taught them that the Bible is the land of milk and honey, the true Promised Land. By the time students graduated from *bet sefer* four years later, they had memorized the entire Torah. Every jot and tittle of Genesis, Exodus, Leviticus, Numbers, and Deuteronomy was engraved on their cerebral cortex via memorization.

After graduating from *bet sefer*, the best students continued on with *bet Talmud* ("house of learning"). From the age of ten to fourteen, students memorized the rest of the Hebrew Scriptures. For what it's worth, I think it's likely that Jesus attended *bet Talmud*. Scripture doesn't explicitly mention it, but even at twelve years of age, Jesus wowed the rabbis in the temple courts with his understanding.

After *bet Talmud*, a select few graduated to *bet midrash* ("house of study"). Those who didn't make the cut would typically go into the family business. Applicants asked a local rabbi if they could be his *talmidim* ("disciples"). If the rabbi chose them, he would extend a verbal invitation: *lech acharai*. Translation: "come, follow me." Inherent within that invitation was an understanding that it meant total surrender, complete devotion. It meant taking that rabbi's yoke on yourself. The yoke represented the sum total of the rabbi's philosophy and practice. It meant spending every waking moment with him. It meant going wherever he went, doing whatever he did, listening to everything he said.

The complete devotion of discipleship is sometimes described as being "covered in the dust of your rabbi." It was an allusion to the fact that disciples followed their rabbi so closely that the dust the rabbi kicked up with his heels would literally cover the disciples who followed him.

The Word of God

One of the surest ways to get into the presence of God is to get into the Word of God. If we get into God's Word, God's Word will get into us. It will radically change the way we think, the way we live, the way we love. But it requires more than a casual reading. In fact, the Bible wasn't meant to be read. It was meant to be memorized and meditated on. It was meant to be prayed and practiced. We have to abide in the Word of God and let the Word of God abide in us.

Words that are repeated throughout Scripture are repeated because they bear repeating. It's God's way of saying, "Don't let this go in one ear and out the other." These are words we need to pay special attention to. One of them is the word *abide*, which is repeated no less than eight times in John 15. In verse 7, John writes, "If you abide in Me, and My words abide in you, ask whatever you wish, and it will be done for you."

The word *abide* is a present imperative verb, which indicates a continual action. It's not something we start and stop; it's something we do for the rest of our lives. And we do more of it. The goal is to get closer and closer to God. And the way we do this is by abiding in His Word.

According to rabbinic tradition, every word of Scripture has seventy faces and six hundred thousand meanings. Each word is kaleidoscopic. And the word *abide* is a great example. Let me turn the kaleidoscope to reveal five reflections of meaning.

To stay overnight. Just like Jesus, who prayed well into the night on the eve of His crucifixion, sometimes we need to press into the presence of God a little longer. And if we linger in His presence, God's presence will linger on us. In my experience, God responds to extra effort with an extra blessing. It's those who spend the most time in God's presence that God can use the most because they are the people He can trust the most.

To hold fast. Every time we pray, we gain a position in the spiritual realm. The kingdom of God is advanced and the forces of darkness must retreat. And our most effective weapon is the Word of God. It's the same weapon Jesus used when He was tempted by Satan. Abiding in the Word of God is the way we take enemy territory and hold our ground. It's our best offense and best defense.

To stand still. Remember when the Israelites found themselves cornered between the Red Sea and the Egyptian army? The Lord spoke to Moses with these words: "Fear ye not, stand still, and see the salvation of the LORD." When we find ourselves between a rock and a hard place, we must stand on the Word of God and trust His promises. We will face some problems we cannot solve, some situations we cannot change. That's when we may feel like panicking, but it is the time to stand still and wait for the Lord's deliverance. No one likes being in those situations, but God often does His most dramatic miracles at those very times.

To be moved. The prophet Haggai writes, "The LORD stirred up the spirit of Zerubbabel." When the Word of God gets in our spirit, which is the spiritual womb, new passions are conceived within us. And inaction is no longer an option. We cannot abide in the Word of God and not be moved to action. We cannot sit on the sidelines. Like David, who ran to the front lines, we'll be looking for giants to conquer.

To tarry. This is precisely what Jesus told His disciples to do after His ascension. Just as they tarried in the upper room for ten days, we must tarry in the Word of God. Perhaps the spiritual disciplines of studying Scripture and engaging in prayer aren't two separate disciplines. One is the key to the other.

We're so busy trying to do something for God that we don't realize that the key to our success in any endeavor is letting God do something for us. We cannot do something *for* God if we aren't *with* God. We have to press into His presence. And the surest way to get into God's presence is by getting into God's Word.

Jewish kings were required to make a personal copy of the law in their own handwriting. They had to keep it on their person wherever they went. I've always found this fascinating. It's something like having a nation's president make a handwritten copy of the constitution and read it every day. So why did God require this of the kings? I think He knew it would force them to internalize it and personalize it. It also served as preventative medicine.

> "This regular reading will prevent him from becoming proud and acting as if he is above his fellow citizens. It will also prevent him from turning away from these commands in the smallest way."

I don't think you need to write out your own personal copy of Scripture, but let me offer one piece of advice that will help you personalize Scripture. Wherever you read the pronoun *you*, insert your name. It will help you take what you read more literally, more personally. It will also remind you that your life is a unique translation of Scripture. If people like what they read in your life, they might just want to pick up the Book that inspired your translation!

*Reading without meditating
is like eating without digesting.*

Spell It Out

"What do you want me to do for you?"
MATTHEW 20:32

More than a thousand years after the original Jeri-cho miracle, another miracle happened in the same place. Jesus was on His way out of the city when two blind men shouted, "Lord, Son of David, have mercy on us!" The disciples saw it as an inconvenient interruption, but divine appointments usually come disguised. The disciples would have walked right past this "miracle waiting to happen." They had places to go and things to do. But Jesus stopped. Then He asked the two men a loaded question: "What do you want me to do for you?"

Is that question even necessary? They are blind. Isn't it obvious what they want? Yet Jesus forced them to define exactly what they wanted from Him. Jesus made them ver-balize it. He made them spell out exactly what they wanted Him to do, but it wasn't because Jesus didn't know what they wanted; He wanted to make sure that they knew what they wanted.

What if Jesus asked you the same question: *What do you*

want Me to do for you? Would you be able to spell out the promises, miracles, and dreams God has put in your heart? I'm afraid many of us would find ourselves at a loss for words. We have no idea what we want God to do for us, and then we wonder why it seems like God isn't doing anything for us. The great irony, of course, is that if we can't answer this question, then we're as blind spiritually as these men were physically.

Most of us don't get what we want simply because we don't know what we want.

We've never made a list of life goals. We've never defined success for ourselves. We've never circled any of God's promises. And we've forgotten most of the prayers we've prayed before they are even answered.

If faith is being sure of what we hope for, then not being sure of what we hope for is the exact opposite of faith, isn't it?

Well-Defined Prayers

A few years ago, I read one sentence that radically affected the way I pray: "God does not answer vague prayers." I was immediately convicted by how vague my prayers were. Some were so vague that there was no way of knowing whether or not God had answered them. To be honest, I was subconsciously hedging my bets. My lack of faith didn't allow me to go out on a limb and lay my true request on the line. And because I was afraid God might not answer, I didn't even give Him a chance to answer!

The more faith we have, the more specific our prayers will be. And the more specific our prayers are, the more glory

God receives. If our prayers aren't specific, however, God gets robbed of the glory He deserves because we second-guess whether or not He actually answered them. We never know if the answers were the result of specific prayers or general coincidences that would have happened anyway. Well-defined prayers give God an opportunity to display His power in new ways. Well-developed faith results in well-defined prayers, and well-defined prayers result in well-defined answers.

Nearly two decades ago, Sergei and Aleona Isakov put their faith in Jesus Christ through the influence of American missionaries who served in Russia. Aleona turned her profession — fashion design — into her pulpit. She has shared her testimony with millions of people by means of televised interviews and live fashion shows in Russia, Israel, England, and Australia. A few years ago, Sergei and Aleona felt called to literally return the favor and move to D.C. as Russian missionaries to America. That's how they landed at National Community Church. In Aleona's words, "We believe that revival is coming to America, and we want to be part of it."

During our prayer challenge, Aleona spelled out six miracles. Their specific nature challenged and inspired me. First, she prayed that God would give her a platform at the National Prayer Breakfast to share her newest fashions. God answered that prayer with an invitation to speak to one hundred guests at the NPB, and one of those guests then invited her to speak at a conference in Norway. Second, they prayed that they'd receive their EB-1 visas, but God did them one better by providing green cards that allow Aleona to bring her entire fashion collection to the United States. Third, she prayed that God would heal her husband's six-month cough. No more cough drops required! Fourth, she prayed that her daughter and son-in-law would get American visas. They got them in two weeks' time. Fifth, she prayed that God would send her a new fashion photographer who loves Jesus. What she didn't expect is that the amazingly talented photographer would volunteer to shoot for free. And last but not least, Aleona prayed for a good job for her husband. Sergei started his job as an IT engineer at *National Geographic Magazine* two days after the prayer challenge ended.

Too often we rob God of the opportunity to answer our prayers because they are so vague. Don't worry about *when* God answers or *how* God answers. That isn't our responsibility. Our responsibility is to simply discern what God wants, and then humbly yet boldly to ask Him for it. And God will throw in a few holy surprises along the way because He may spell the answer differently than we spelled the request.

The Ladder of Success

Jesus is still asking the question: *What do you want Me to do for you?* And like the two blind men outside Jericho, we still need an encounter with the Son of God. We need an answer to the question. We need to identify our Jericho — the promise we are circling.

What promise are you praying around? What miracle are you marching around? What dream does your life revolve around?

What is your Jericho?

Jericho is spelled many different ways. If a loved one has cancer, it's spelled *healing*. If your best friend is far from God, it's spelled *salvation*. If your family is falling apart, it's spelled *reconciliation*. If you have a dream beyond your finances, it's spelled *provision*. But whatever it is, you have to spell it out.

It's easy to get so busy climbing the ladder of success that we fail to realize the ladder is not leaning against the wall of Jericho. Eternal priorities get overshadowed by our everyday responsibilities, and we pawn our God-given dream for the American dream. So instead of circling Jericho, we end up wandering in the wilderness.

What is your Jericho?

If you can't answer this question, stop reading. Get into God's presence and get an answer! Obviously, the answer to this question changes over time. We need different miracles during different seasons of life. We pursue different dreams during different stages of life. And we stake claim to different promises during different situations. It's a moving target, but we have to start somewhere.

Why not right here, right now?

Define your dream. Claim your promise. Spell your miracle.

Draw the Circle

Most of us don't get what we want because we don't know what we want.

Get a Testimony

"... and by the word of their testimony ..."
REVELATION 12:11

Since the release of *The Circle Maker*, I've become a connoisseur of prayer testimonies. Hardly a day goes by that I don't hear a story that makes me want to cry or give God a round of applause. Those testimonies have lit a fire under my faith unlike anything I've ever experienced. Here's why: *If God did it for them, He might just do it for me.* Maybe that's why Revelation 12:11 places such importance on sharing testimonies. And maybe that's why the enemy wants us to keep our testimonies silent.

> "They triumphed over him
> by the blood of the Lamb
> and by the word of their testimony."

When God answers a prayer, no matter how big or how small, we need to share it. It's a stewardship issue. If we don't turn the answer to prayer into praise, it may very well turn into pride. Giving testimony is the way we give God all of the glory. But we also need to share it because others need to hear it. If we don't share our testimonies of how God is working in our lives, then others are tempted to think He isn't working at all.

Jesus triumphed over the enemy by His shed blood on Calvary's cross. He broke the curse of sin so we can break the cycle of sin. But the way we seal the victory is through our testimonies. Our testimonies don't just remind us that the victory has already been won; they also remind the enemy that he has already been defeated.

I wonder if the lack of awe in many churches is directly attributable to the lost art of the testimony. Churches that see people radically saved are usually churches that allow radically saved people to share their testimonies. Is it any wonder that what gets celebrated gets replicated? When a testimony of healing is shared, for example, those who hear it get an infusion of faith to believe God for healing in their own lives. Those testimonies double as prophecies!

When we share a testimony, we are loaning our faith to others. When we listen to a testimony, we are borrowing faith from others. Either way, the church is edified and God is glorified.

Hearsay

In the worlds of criminal law and academic research, we see a big difference between first-person and second-person testimony. A first-person witness is more credible because they actually saw it with their own eyes. Second-person testimony is hearsay. It doesn't mean it's not true; it just means it doesn't hold as much weight.

A testimony is powerful, in part, because we cannot argue with it. It's irrefutable and undeniable. A personal testimony is our secret weapon, and that's why the enemy wants us to keep our testimony a secret. It's not a testimony if we don't share it with others. If we don't share our testimonies, we are robbing God of the glory He deserves. And we aren't just holding out on God; we are holding out on those who need to hear it.

Our churches are filled with hearsay. What we need are witnesses with first-person testimonies. No amount of education can compensate for a lack of first-person experience. We don't get a testimony in seminary; we get a testimony by being tested. And if we pass the test, we get a testimony. That testimony is worth far more than any seminary degree can afford. And that first-person experience with God will override any of our inadequacies. Peter and John were described as "unschooled, ordinary men," yet the Jewish council was amazed at their boldness. It simply says that "they took note that these men had been with Jesus."

Nothing can compare to the power of first-person testimony. The most educated and erudite second-person testimony still can't compare with a first-person witness! So go ahead and get an education. Study to present yourself to God as one approved. But please don't just get an education; get a testimony! We don't change the world by going to graduate school or getting a degree. If we want to change the world, we must spend a lot of time with Jesus.

Remember the Samaritan woman who was totally transformed by a single encounter with Jesus at the well? She went back to her village and shared her testimony. That testimony sparked faith in those who heard, but their faith was secondhand faith. They needed their own encounter with Jesus, and that's exactly what they got. The transition from secondhand to firsthand faith is evidenced in their words: "Now we believe, not just because of what you told us, but because we have heard him ourselves."

We cannot live off of someone else's experience forever. Secondhand faith is as dangerous as secondhand smoke. We need a faith with our own name on it. We need to own it, and it needs to own us. We can't just know *what* we believe; we need to know *why* we believe what we believe. And it must be continually upgraded.

Don't be satisfied with simply going to church; get into God's presence.

Don't be satisfied with hearsay; get a word from the Lord.

Don't be satisfied with secondhand faith; get a testimony!

Crazy Prayers

One of my pastor friends, and a local hero, is Mike Minter. Mike is the founding pastor of Reston Bible Church, where he has served for nearly four decades. One day over coffee, Mike told me about a missionary friend named Jamie Winship, whose mission field is the Muslim world. Jamie travels to Baghdad frequently. He knows the Qur'an backward and forward. And he has led countless imams to faith in Jesus Christ.

Jamie is one of those guys who prays crazy prayers and

then crazy stuff happens. Divine appointments happen right and left. He'll be praying for a particular imam, and that imam will just happen to be on the same plane going to the same place or in the same restaurant at the table right behind him.

One morning Mike was scheduled to have breakfast with Jamie, so he prayed, "Lord, I'm sick of just hearing stories; I want to see one. Do something sovereign that is unmistakable." When they got in line to place their order, Mike noticed that the woman in front of them was wearing the traditional Muslim *hijab* with head covering. All they could see was the woman's eyes. Jamie greeted her in Arabic, which got her attention. Then he said, "I know you." Even though he could see only her eyes, he said, "I heard you speak at the University of Georgia a year ago" — to which she responded, "I remember you. You sat on the front row."

Not only was this woman one of the most influential Muslim women in the world, but Jamie had been praying for her by name. In fact, he had been praying that he would meet her, but he didn't know how to contact her. She happened to be in D.C. from out of town, and evidently God knew they both liked Panera Bread. As a result of the meeting, this woman contacted a number of leading imams, who met with Mike and Jamie to dialogue about faith.

I think Jamie's prayer, coupled with Mike's prayer for something sovereign to happen, collided at Panera.

That is a divine appointment of biblical proportions! And it reveals the power of two people praying. You never know when your prayer will collide with someone else's prayer and result in a miracle. But this is what happened with Mike and Jamie. They tag-teamed in prayer, and it resulted in a supernatural synchronicity. You can call me a simpleton, but I believe that God is still seated on His throne. And if God is ordering my footsteps, and I believe He is, then He is going to make sure I get where I need to go and meet whomever I need to meet.

I hope this testimony to God's sovereignty is encouraging, but it's also meant to be an exhortation. Mike wasn't satisfied with simply hearing someone else's story. Secondhand faith wasn't enough. There comes a point when you, like Mike, grow weary of hearing other people's stories. You need a story of your own. It's got to have your name on it. You've got to see it, hear it, taste it, feel it, touch it, and smell it for yourself.

You need to go get a testimony! Then you need to share it.

Draw the Circle

Most of us are educated way beyond the level of our obedience.

Prayer Covering

Aaron and Hur held his hands up —
one on one side, one on the other.
EXODUS 17:12

During my first decade of pastoring in D.C., I often felt like the Lone Ranger. I was doing my thing my way. I was so busy trying to build our church that I forfeited potential friendships with other local pastors. Then one day the Lord convicted me that it was easier for me to pray for a church four states away than a church four blocks away. So I started praying for area churches. We started investing in local church plants, and I started inviting local pastors to share their stories and their hearts with our team during staff devotions. Many of those staff meetings turned into prayer meetings. We would inevitably end up on our knees interceding for each other. Each time a local pastor did devotions, I felt the stronghold of territorialism being weakened.

I firmly believe we need many different kinds of churches because there are many different kinds of people. As long as a church is preaching the gospel, it's all for one and one for all. We may have different church names over the door, but there is one church and one Shepherd of the church. So I'm praying for revival in our nation's capital, but it doesn't have to start with National Community Church. I just want in on it.

In the last few years, God has blessed us with some tremendous pastor friends. Lora has cultivated friendships with four pastors' wives — Donna, Heather, Jill, and Taryn. And I've cultivated friendships with a handful of pastors whom I've grown to love and respect as brothers and fathers in the faith. Even pastors need pastors, and the Lord has blessed me with an Aaron and a Hur.

Bob Mathieu and Michael Hall have pastored in D.C. almost as long as I've been alive. Without my knowledge, they covenanted together to circle me in prayer every day. It's hard to describe what it means to have two seventy-something pastors praying for me daily, but I feel those prayers lifting up my arms.

Part of what makes these newfound friendships so meaningful is that they are the answer to a prayer I didn't even know was being prayed. A member of my prayer circle recently revealed that they had been specifically praying for God to strategically place older pastors in my life. Over the last few years, God has answered those prayers. The answers are spelled Michael, Bob, Amos, Mike, Stuart, Dennis, and Glenn, just to name a few.

Aaron and Hur

If we are going to intercede for others, we had better be sure that others are interceding for us. We need a prayer covering, especially when we enter an intense season of prayer and fasting. When we hit our knees, we pick a fight with the enemy. And the enemy will fight back. Make no mistake, there is a target on our back. The enemy wants to take us out, but he cannot touch us. He has no jurisdiction in our lives if we are covered by the blood of Jesus, but we also need a prayer covering.

Intercession is spiritual warfare. It's not for the faint or the feeble. By definition, praying hard is hard. There will be times when our hearts are breaking because of a prayer burden. There will be seasons when the labor pains become intense because the Holy Spirit is birthing something new in us. And there will be times when we feel the enemy launching a frontal assault on our family or business or church. That's when we need to stay on our knees and pray through.

Spiritual warfare can be scary and lonely, but I've always been strangely encouraged when I encounter increased spiritual opposition or oppression. It means I'm doing something right. It means I'm riling up the enemy. It's means I'm inching closer to the breakthrough. And just when the fighting gets fiercest, I know that God is getting ready to go to battle for me.

In Exodus 17, we find a blow-by-blow description of an ancient battle between the Israelites and the Amalekites. As long as Moses was lifting up his arms, the Israelites were gaining ground. But when Moses grew tired and lowered his arms, the Israelites lost ground. That's when Aaron and Hur stood alongside Moses and lifted up his arms until sunset.

Spiritual battles are fought the same way. The victory is

won with knees bent in prayer and hands raised in worship to God. The enemy cannot be defeated any other way. No victory has ever been won apart from prayer and praise.

We will have moments when we lack the ability, strength, will, or faith to pray for ourselves. That's when we need a prayer partner or prayer circle to hold up our arms, just as Aaron and Hur did for Moses. I'm so grateful for my personal prayer circle. There are a lot of people who pray for my family, but I have an inner circle that prays with a little more specificity, consistency, and intensity. I know they are on their knees interceding for me every day. I may unfairly get credit for the things I have done, but they get the assist.

Footnotes

The day after the Israelites defeated the Amalekites, I'm sure Moses made the headlines. But in the grand scheme of God's story, there is a footnote behind every headline. The footnote is prayer. And the true heroes of the kingdom are the Aarons and the Hurs.

In the words of Walter Wink, "History belongs to the intercessors."

Charles Finney was the most famous evangelist of his generation. He made headlines during the Second Great Awakening, but there is a footnote to the story. Finney had an "Aaron" named Daniel Nash. At the age of forty-eight, Father Nash quit his pastorate to devote himself to full-time intercession. Several weeks before Finney would visit a city, Father Nash would rent a room, recruit two or three intercessors, and begin laying a prayer foundation for the revival that would follow. By the time Finney showed up, the hard work had already been done. The victory had already been secured in the spiritual realm.

During one of his revivals, Finney was contacted by a woman who ran a boarding house in town. She asked him, "Brother Finney, do you know a Father Nash? He and two other men have been at my boarding house for the last three days, but they haven't eaten a bite of food. I opened the door and peeped in at them because I could hear them groaning, and I saw them down on their faces. They have been this way for three days, lying prostrate on the floor and groaning. I thought something awful must have happened to them. I was afraid to go in, and I didn't know what to do. Would you please come see about them?" Finney replied, "No, it isn't necessary. They just have a spirit of travail in prayer."

When public meetings started, Father Nash rarely attended. He stayed in his prayer closet pleading with God for the convicting power of the Holy Spirit to fall on the crowd and melt their hearts.

Shortly before his death in 1831, Father Nash recorded these words in his journal.

I am now convinced; it is my duty and privilege, and the duty of every other Christian, to pray for as much of the Holy Spirit as came down on the day of Pentecost, and a great deal more ... I have only just begun to understand what Jesus meant when He said, "All things whatsoever ye shall ask in prayer, believing, ye shall receive."

Father Nash is buried in a small cemetery near the border of New York and Canada. The headstone on his grave contains the following epitaph:

DANIEL NASH
Laborer with Finney
Mighty in Prayer
Nov. 17, 1775 — Dec. 20, 1831

Prayer is the pen that writes history. Don't worry about making headlines; focus on the footnotes. And if you focus on the footnotes, God will write the headlines.

If you intercede for others,
make sure others are interceding for you.

Raise Up a Remnant

And the remnant shall yet again take root
downward, and bear fruit upward.
2 KINGS 19:30 KJV

In the eighteenth century, Count Nikolaus Ludwig von Zinzendorf formed a holy conspiracy called "the Order of the Mustard Seed." Members wore a ring inscribed with the motto "none live for themselves." They solemnly pledged to be true to Christ, to be kind to people, and to take the gospel to the nations. The secret order included such notables as the king of Denmark, the Anglican archbishop of Canterbury, the secretary of state of Scotland, and the eighty-seven-year-old Creek Indian chief Tomochichi.

On the evening before the order was formed, Zinzendorf called his friends to prayer. He held up the ring and said, "Brothers, we know why we are here. Tomorrow we will make our covenant, but tonight let us pray." Zinzendorf himself prayed all night. The next morning they pledged to use all of their gifts, all of their wealth, and all of their influence for the conversion of the heathen. Zinzendorf then laid hands on each member of the order and individually prayed for them.

The ceremony lasted a few minutes, but the covenant lasted a lifetime.

What was begun that day culminated in the Moravian Pentecost at Herrnhut in 1727. On August 27 of that year, a small remnant of twenty-four brothers and twenty-four sisters began praying around the clock. That prayer meeting was visited by the Holy Spirit, not unlike the 120 who prayed in the upper room on the day of Pentecost. Thus began hourly intercessions that would not stop for one hundred years! Even the children of the village formed prayer circles. And those prayers reverberated all around the world in one of the greatest missionary movements the church has ever known. Thousands of missionaries were called and commissioned. Some even sold themselves into slavery in order to reach their mission field.

Reformation

At critical junctures in history, God raises up a remnant to reestablish His reign and rule. It's rarely a majority. In fact, it's almost always a small minority. But all it takes is a faithful few to begin a reformation.

It's not a new discovery that sparks it. Reformations are birthed out of rediscovering something ancient, something simple, something true. In the days of Hilkiah the priest, for example, it was the rediscovery of the Book of the Law that sparked national revival. That one rediscovery brought a nation to its knees.

Every generation needs a reformation. Every generation

needs to tear down its idols and rebuild its temples. Every generation needs to repent of its sin and rediscover the ancient truths.

During our forty-day challenge at National Community Church, we felt we needed to circle one promise for forty days.

> "If my people, who are called by my name, will humble themselves and pray and seek my face and turn from their wicked ways, then I will hear from heaven, and I will forgive their sin and will heal their land."

If we circle the promises of God, God will deliver on them. It's not a question of *if*; it's only a question of *when*. But if we are determined to pray as long as it takes, revival will come. It's as predictable as the sun rising in the east. It's as inevitable as the sun setting into the west.

In the words of Charles Finney, "God is one pent-up revival."

And all it takes is a remnant rising up!

As a reminder of the promise, our church started gathering at 7:14 a.m. for corporate prayer. When the clock hit 7:14, we hit our knees. It became as instinctual as hunger pangs. Not getting on our knees felt like missing a meal.

It was at 7:14 a.m. on the National Day of Prayer that I felt as though the Spirit of God gave me a word: *I'm raising up a remnant.* To be honest, I was a little discouraged on that particular morning that we didn't have more people at our prayer meeting! After all, it was the National Day of Prayer. But that's when God reminded me that all it takes is a rem-

nant. I stopped worrying about who had or hadn't shown up.
I started focusing on the promise of exponential potential
when just two or three pray in His name!

I believe there is a remnant within every church, within
every city. It's time to rise up. It's time for reformation. The
next great awakening won't be the result of a planning meeting. Just as it was for Pentecost, it will be birthed in a prayer
meeting.

Since the National Day of Prayer, I've been circling 2 Kings
19:30. I believe it's a promise for our generation, for every
generation.

> "Once more a remnant of the kingdom of Judah
> will take root below and bear fruit above."

We will bear fruit above! Heaven will be populated because
of our prayers. But the root of revival is prayer. We've got to
press into the presence of God as never before. Like the members of the Order of the Mustard Seed, we must covenant to
seek God with all our heart and soul.

An Eviction Notice

In the 1950s, Argentina was a spiritual wasteland. According
to Dr. Edward Miller, a missionary who spent four decades
in Argentina, there were only six hundred Spirit-filled believ-
ers in the entire country. In his book *Cry for Me Argentina*,
he describes the genesis of a revival that started in Argentina
and swept across South America.

It began with fifty students at the Argentine Bible Institute who developed an intense prayer burden for the nation of Argentina. Dr. Miller said he had never seen people weep so hard or pray so long. Day after day, they wept and prayed. After hours of intercession, students would literally be standing in their own puddle of tears.

On the fiftieth day of around-the-clock intercession, there was a prophetic word. "Weep no more, for the Lion of the tribe of Judah hath prevailed over the prince of Argentina." Eighteen months later, hundreds of thousands of Argentines were flocking to crusades at soccer stadiums. The largest stadiums, seating 180,000 people, weren't large enough to handle the crowds.

Dr. Miller came to this conclusion:

> If God can get enough people in an area to reject the rulership and the dominion of satan, if enough of His people will reject satan's dominion in the right way — with humility, with brokenness, and in repentant intercession — then God will slap an eviction notice on the doorway of the ruling demonic power of that area. And when He does, then there is a light and glory that begins to come.

We never know how or when or where a move of God might begin. But if we hit our knees, God will extend His mighty right hand on our behalf. If we lay a foundation of prayer, God will build something spectacular on top of it. If we intercede like never before, God will intervene like never before.

When the prayer meeting becomes the most important meeting, revival is around the corner.

The Longest Lever

"Do not despise these small beginnings."
ZECHARIAH 4:10 NLT

On July 1, 1857, Jeremiah Lanphier was called to be a city missionary in New York City. He soon felt led to begin a daily meeting where businesspeople in New York City could gather for midday prayer. The first meeting was held in September in the upper room of the consistory building of the Dutch Reformed Church in Manhattan. Only six people showed up. The following week there were fourteen. The week after that there were twenty-three. Eventually the prayer meeting expanded into the main sanctuary of the church and then outgrew the church itself. The prayer meetings began to multiply across the city until daily gatherings for prayer took place in almost every public building in New York City.

Commenting on Jonathan Edwards's call to "a visible union of God's people in extraordinary prayer," J. Edwin Orr writes, "When people are found getting up at six in the morning to pray, or having a half night of prayer until midnight, or giving up their lunch time to pray at a noonday prayer meeting, that is extraordinary prayer."

Horace Greeley, founder of the most influential newspaper of its day, the *New-York Tribune*, sent one of his reporters to investigate the growing revival. The reporter visited twelve prayer meetings in one hour on one day and counted 6,100 men fervently seeking God in prayer. At the peak of the revival, it is estimated that nearly 10,000 people were converted every week in New York City, roughly 1 percent of the population of one million per week!

I'd like to know who those six people were at the first prayer meeting. I can't help but wonder if they were discouraged that first week. Did they have any inkling they were starting something that would impact hundreds of thousands of lives? I have a hunch they had no clue. Very rarely does anyone know they are making history while they are making it. And that isn't our job anyway. But if we pray like the members of the early church did, Pentecost can happen anywhere. Our prayers have the potential to write and rewrite history.

Small Beginnings

In Zechariah 4, the Jewish remnant who returned to Israel are getting ready to rebuild the temple. It is an overwhelming undertaking. But the Lord encourages them with these words:

> "Do not despise these small beginnings, for the LORD rejoices to see the work begin, to see the plumb line in Zerubbabel's hand."

The plumb line was an ancient measuring tape. All they

had done at this point was measure! That's it. But God was already rejoicing over them. Like a parent that celebrates a baby's first step, our heavenly Father rejoices when we take the smallest of steps in the right direction. And those small steps become giant leaps in God's kingdom. If we do little things, God will do the big things. But we have to do the little things *like* they are big things.

We cannot worry about what we cannot do; we have to simply do what we can.

Oswald Chambers once wrote, "It is inbred in us that we have to do exceptional things for God; but we have not. We have to be exceptional in the ordinary things." And if we do the ordinary, God will add an extra to it.

Prayer is our plumb line. It's also the true measure of a person. No one is greater than their prayer life. Our potential is directly proportional to our prayer life. It is the single greatest indicator of our success in any endeavor.

The Lever

Archimedes of Syracuse is famous for his quip, "Give me a place to stand on, and I will move the earth." He was referencing the lever, one of six simple machines identified by Renaissance scientists. A lever amplifies the input force to provide a greater output force. Simply put, the longer the lever, the greater the leverage.

Let me borrow this simple statement and substitute one word: *Give me a place to kneel on, and I will move the earth.* In the kingdom of God, humility equals authority. Call it bold humility or humble boldness. That is our lever. If we try to exalt ourselves, God will find a way to humble us. But if we humble ourselves, God will find a way to exalt us. There is no leverage like kneeling in prayer. If we hit our knees in humble prayer, God will extend His mighty hand on our behalf. He will leverage us in ways that are humanly impossible.

One of our mantras at NCC is "stay humble, stay hungry." Humility is how we get out of the way of what God wants to do. And if we stay out of God's way, then there is nothing God cannot do in us and through us.

The first thing I do every day is hit my knees — a daily ritual that began the day we started our forty-day prayer challenge. At the end of those forty days, I was a totally different person. I have no idea why I wasn't kneeling every morning before that, but when those forty days concluded, I couldn't imagine starting my day any other way. There is nothing magical about kneeling, but there is something biblical about it. Posturing our bodies helps us posture our hearts. Bowing our hearts in reverence before God is what really matters, but I've found that it's easier to do if I'm in a kneeling position.

During our forty-day prayer challenge, God revealed his favor in amazing ways. We received the kind of news coverage that money cannot buy. *The Washington Post* ran a remarkably positive front-page story in the weekend Metro section. A few weeks later, the *Today Show* filmed one of our weekend services, and the segment aired on the last day of our forty-day prayer challenge. Coincidence? I think not. It had God's fingerprints of favor all over it.

Publicity isn't something to be sought, but it is something

we must steward. To be honest, it's a two-edged sword. The more publicity you get, the more you get pelted with stones. So on a personal level, I am inclined to avoid it at all costs. It just complicates my life. But if God can be glorified through it, then so be it. And I do believe that the good news ought to make the news. God was glorified through the *Today Show* segment that aired on Easter Sunday, and many unchurched folks have visited our church as a result. So praise God!

One of the unexpected blessings was ministering to the film crew. The reporter who did the story told me that her father was an atheist, but she had a praying grandmother. I gave Maria a copy of *The Circle Maker*. A few weeks later, she told me it was revolutionizing her prayer life. She even bought copies for some of her friends and family members. Who knows, maybe God is raising up a remnant at NBC!

Draw
the
Circle

If we do the ordinary,
God will add an extra to it.

Senior Partner

"Store up for yourselves treasures in heaven."
MATTHEW 6:20

I have a ninety-five-year-old friend named Stanley Tam. Actually, he's more than a friend; Stanley is one of my heroes. More than a half century ago, he made a decision to make God his Senior Partner. In one of the most unique corporate takeovers ever, Stanley legally transferred 51 percent of his business to God.

Stanley started the United States Plastic Corporation with $37 in capital. When he gave his business over to God, annual revenues were less than $200,000, but Stanley believed God would bless his business, and he wanted to honor God from the get-go.

At that point, most of us would have been patting ourselves on the back, but not Stanley. He felt convicted for keeping 49 percent for himself. After reading the parable about the merchant who found the pearl of great price and sold everything he had to obtain it, Stanley made a decision to divest himself of all his shares.

On January 15, 1955, every share of stock was transferred to his Senior Partner, and Stanley became a salaried employee of the company he had started. Since the day Stanley made that defining decision, he has given away more than $120 million.

Stanley spoke at National Community Church a few years ago, and afterward we shared one of the most memorable meals I've ever had. I ate up every word that came out of his mouth. The wisdom he dispensed in one hour will last a lifetime. In his matter-of-fact manner, Stanley said, "God's shovel is always bigger than ours." Translation: "We cannot outgive God." Stanley discovered the key that unlocks the joy of generosity: what we keep we ultimately lose; what we give away we ultimately get back. So Stanley said, "I just send it ahead by giving it away." Then Stanley threw out a one-liner that is more insightful than anything I've learned in the process of gaining three seminary degrees: "God cannot reward Abraham yet because his seed is still multiplying."

The same is true of Stanley. It will take quite a while to calculate his reward in heaven — not because of the amount given but because of the percentage. Stanley came awfully close to giving away 100 percent. As Stanley puts it, "A man can eat only one meal at a time, wear only one suit of clothes at a time, drive only one car at a time. All this I have. Isn't that enough?"

The Same God

Toward the end of our meal, Stanley shared one last thought that doubled as dessert. I'm not sure if it's *what* he said or *how* he said it, but it struck me as a simple profundity. Stanley said, "I've got the same God that George Müller has."

The same God who helped George Müller raise tens of millions of dollars is the same God who helped Stanley Tam give away tens of millions of dollars! And He's the same God who can accomplish the plans and purposes He has put in your heart. If it's God-ordained, it's inevitable.

Few things are as inspiring as seeing childlike faith in a very old person. That's Stanley Tam. He is the youngest oldest person I know. He simply takes God at His word. And when we take God at His word, God stands by His word.

One of the mistakes we make in reading history, whether biblical history or history in general, is thinking that those who lived before us were different from us. They weren't. If God did it for them, He can do it for us. And if we do what they did in the Bible, I'm convinced that God will do what He did. Nothing has changed. God wants to renew His deeds in our day. But we need to pray the price. Leonard Ravenhill put it this way:

> One of these days some simple soul will pick up the Book of God, read it, *and believe it*. Then the rest of us will be embarrassed. We have adopted the convenient theory that the Bible is a Book to be explained, whereas first and foremost it is a Book to be believed (and after that to be obeyed).

Legacy

I recently had the privilege of speaking at a conference hosted by a wonderful organization called Generous Giving. The focus of this annual gathering of some of the wealthiest Christians in the country is giving generously and strategically to kingdom causes. While there, I met some members of the Maclellan Family Foundation. They are among the most respected philanthropists in the world, and leaders in the generosity movement.

On June 7, 1857, a Scotsman named Thomas Maclellan made a covenant with the All in All. That covenant, made on his twentieth birthday, was renewed on his fiftieth and seventieth birthdays. More than five generations later, the seeds he sowed are still multiplying in the millions of dollars that are given away. But the genealogy of generosity traces back to one defining prayer.

> I now fall down before Thy throne and prostrate myself at Thy footstool ... O God of Heaven, record it in the book of Thy remembrances that from henceforth I am Thine forever. I renounce all former lords that have had dominion over me and consecrate all that I am and all that I have, the faculties of my mind, the members of my body, my worldly possessions, my time, and my influence over others, all to be used entirely for Thy glory and resolutely employed in obedience to Thy commands as long as Thou continuest me in life.

The greatest legacy a person can leave is a complete surrender of their life to the lordship of Jesus Christ. If we don't hold out on God, God won't hold out on us. Take God at His promise as expressed by the psalmist: "No good thing does He withhold from those who walk uprightly." And these good things will pass from generation to generation and become great things. God will answer our prayers in the lives of offspring we won't meet until the Father's family reunion at the marriage supper of the Lamb. But every prayer we pray, every gift we give, every sacrifice we make, and every step of faith we take is an inheritance left to the next generation. And our prayers live on, long after we die, in their lives.

What we keep we ultimately lose;
what we give away we ultimately get back.

Day 37

Prayer Contracts

"Whatever you bind on earth
will be bound in heaven."
MATTHEW 18:18

More than a decade ago, I walked by a crack house on Capitol Hill, and God gave me a vision for a coffeehouse. It was a ridiculous prayer at that point because we had hardly any money and hardly any people. So we just kept walking around it the way the Israelites circled Jericho. Over the course of five years, we must have laid hands on it, stood on it, and circled it ten thousand times!

The owner's original asking price was $1 million, but the more we prayed, the more the price dropped. By the time we purchased it, we got it for $325,000. The amazing thing, however, is that four different parties offered more money for it than we did, including two real estate developers.

So how did we get it? My only explanation is Matthew 18:18: "Whatever you bind on earth will be bound in heaven." Our prayers were hyperlinked to that promise. We genuinely believed that our vision was given by God. Just as Jesus hung out at wells — a natural gathering place in the ancient world

—we wanted to create a postmodern well where the church and community could cross paths. And this piece of property —one block from Union Station, kitty-corner to the Securities and Exchange Commission, and right in the heart of historic Capitol Hill—was our Promised Land.

The word *bind* has a legal connotation. It means "to place a contract on something." This is precisely what happens when we pray in the will of God. Our prayers place a contract in the spiritual realm. So while February 7, 2002, is the date we put signatures on a piece of paper and took ownership of the property in the eyes of the government, the spiritual contract predates it by several years. The deal dates back to the first prayer circle we drew around the property.

Full Authority

I've emphasized a simple truth throughout this book, and I'd like to say it one more time for good measure: the purpose of prayer is not to get what you want; the goal of prayer is to discern what God wants, what God wills. But if your prayer is in the will of God, then it is backed by the full authority of the King and His kingdom.

A. W. Tozer wrote, "What comes into our minds when we think about God is the most important thing about us." So let me ask the question: When you think about God, what images come into your mind? The image that comes into my mind is a picture of Jesus with a lamb draped around his shoulders, because that is the painting that hung in my grandparents' house. For most people, I suspect the dominant image is Jesus hanging on a cross. That gruesome cross is the most beautiful picture of what true love looks like. But let me make an observation that may sound a bit sacrilegious. You aren't praying to a God who is hanging on a cross; Jesus is seated on the throne, and the earth is His footstool. All authority is His. And if you are His, then His authority is yours.

We grossly underestimate the authority that is ours because we are children of God. And we desperately need a vision like the one Isaiah had, who saw the Lord high and lifted up.

I think Tozer was right when he stated that a low view of God is the cause of a hundred lesser evils and a high view of God is the solution to ten thousand problems. Our biggest problem is our small view of God. God is so much bigger than our biggest problems. God is so much better than our best thoughts. He is infinitely wiser and more gracious and powerful than anything we can imagine.

Negotiate

In retrospect, I'm glad it took as long as it did to purchase our piece of our Promised Land. And I'm glad it was as hard as it was. Why? Because we learned to dream big, pray hard, and think long. It may sound redundant, but if it hadn't taken a miracle, it wouldn't be a miracle.

That experience didn't just teach us how to negotiate on a human plane; it taught us how to negotiate with God through intercession. It pushed our limits and stretched our faith. And now we're stewarding the miracle by believing God for even bigger and better miracles.

We tend to view the goal as the goal, but in God's economy, the process is the goal. It's not about *what* we're doing at all; it's about *who* we're becoming in the process.

It's not about doing great things for God; it's about God doing great things in us.

After explaining the binding nature of our prayers, Jesus explains the power of prayer circles.

> "If two of you agree on earth about anything that they may ask, it shall be done for them by My Father who is in heaven. For where two or three have gathered together in My name, I am there in their midst."

The concept of prayer circles is a double entendre. It refers to specific things we are circling in prayer, like the crack house that we turned into our coffeehouse. But when two or three agree in prayer, they are forming a prayer circle around the prayer circle. It's like double or triple circling!

The word *bind* means "to tie together." It's the same word used to describe marriage vows. Just as the two become one flesh, when we agree in prayer, the two become one spirit.

Something powerful happens when we agree in prayer. Our faith isn't just added together; it's multiplied. It doesn't mean we can walk down to our local car dealership and circle our favorite model with some friends. But if we are praying in the will of God and for the glory of God, then agreeing with someone in prayer is like getting our prayer contract notarized.

Finally, the word *bind* means "to chain." There are more than three thousand promises in Scripture, and according to the apostle Paul, all of them "are 'Yes' in Christ." Our most powerful prayers are chained to the promises of God. Don't just pray your words all the time; pray the Word of God because His word does not return to Him empty.

In the Old Testament, the idea of binding yourself to the Word of God was taken literally. The Word of God was kept in visible places and attached to body parts as a constant reminder. The Lord commanded the Israelites, "Thou shalt bind them for a sign upon thine hand, and they shall be as frontlets between thine eyes."

Chain it to your mind through memorization. Chain it to your heart through meditation. Chain it to your past, present, and future through prayer.

Agreeing with someone in prayer is like getting your prayer notarized.

Climb the Watchtower

I will climb up to my watchtower
and stand at my guardpost.
HABAKKUK 2:1 NLT

Watchtowers served a variety of purposes in ancient culture — as built-in defense systems in the walls of ancient cities, as built-in pastures so shepherds could protect their flocks from wild animals, and as built-in vineyards for protection from thieves. Watchmen would climb into their watchtower, station themselves at their guardpost, and scan the horizon for enemy armies or trading caravans. The watchmen were the first to see, and they saw the farthest. So it is with those who pray. Intercessors are watchmen and watchwomen. They see sooner and see farther in the spiritual realm. Why? Because prayer gives us a unique vantage point.

My watchtower is Ebenezer's Coffeehouse. I love praying on the rooftop because I'm praying on top of an answered prayer. I often climb the ladder, pop the hatch, and pace back and forth in prayer. It's hard *not* to pray with faith when we pray in a place where God has already done a miracle.

I wonder if that is how Elijah felt as he prayed for rain on top of Mount Carmel. God had just answered an impossible prayer on that very mountain. Elijah defeated the 450 prophets of Baal in a sudden-death showdown on Mount Carmel. The God who sent *fire* can certainly send *rain*, right? That miracle gave Elijah the faith he needed to pray hard. And that is one of the by-products of answered prayer. It gives us the faith to believe God for bigger and better miracles. With each answered prayer, we draw bigger prayer circles. With each act of faithfulness, it increases our faith. With each promise kept, it increases our persistence quotient.

Geography and spirituality are not unrelated. That's why the Israelites built memorials in places of spiritual significance. During seasons of repentance, they would often return to those ancient altars to renew their covenant with God.

I have to believe that David revisited more than once the battlefield where he defeated Goliath. That Abraham made a pilgrimage back to the thicket where God provided a ram. That Peter rowed out to the place on the Sea of Galilee where he walked on water — and it renewed his faith. That Paul built a personal altar on the road to Damascus where God knocked him off his high horse. And that Zacchaeus let his grandkids climb the sycamore-fig tree where he had gotten his first glimpse of Jesus.

Going back to places of spiritual significance should be part of our spiritual rhythm. I occasionally go back to the cow pasture in Alexandria, Minnesota, where I felt called to ministry. I go back to the chapel balcony at my alma mater where I learned to pray. I go back to the places that remind me of God's faithfulness because they renew my faith.

For that reason, and a hundred others, *where* we pray is not insignificant. The Israelites pitched the tent of meeting outside the camp for a reason. Jesus prayed on mountains, by water, and in gardens for a reason. We need to find a place where we are free from distraction, where we get good reception, where we can focus, and where our faith is strong.

Prayer Targets

One ancient translation of Habakkuk 2:1 reads, "I will stand upon my watch, and station me within a circle." This Scripture inspired Honi to draw a circle in the sand and pray for rain. Honi stationed himself within the circle by kneeling inside it and praying the prayer that saved a generation: "Lord of the universe, I swear before Your great name that I will not move from this circle until You have shown mercy upon Your children." Honi was willing to die within that circle!

Once again, there is nothing magical about circling something in prayer, but there is something biblical about it. There are times when we have to mark God's territory. We have to pray a perimeter around a promise God has put in our heart. We have to be willing to go in and not come out until God answers.

Doing so can take a hundred different forms. Let me share a few examples.

I recently spoke at the weekly prayer meeting at Christ Tabernacle in Queens, New York. Michael and Maria Durso founded Christ Tab, a daughter church of Brooklyn Tabernacle, nearly three decades ago. Their three sons, Adam,

Jordan, and Chris, are on the pastoral staff, and they are one of the most anointed families I've ever met. This anointing is a testament to the power of prayer because all three boys were prodigals as teenagers. At times, it seemed as though their sons were lost beyond lost, but Michael and Maria would not stop fasting and praying for them. They literally purchased a shooting target, wrote their boys' names on the bull's-eye, and kept aiming their intercessions at their boys. That target was a tangible way of drawing a circle around them. It took years of circling, and they experienced seasons of discouragement, but one by one their boys came back to Christ.

One footnote.

When Michael and Maria were in their twenties, they were as far from God as a person can get. They lived from drug fix to drug fix, and they mocked anything remotely religious. They were on vacation when Maria mysteriously came under the conviction of the Holy Spirit. She wasn't in church. She wasn't listening to a preacher. She wasn't reading a Bible. The conviction came out of nowhere. What she didn't know is that thirty of her friends had gotten saved after she and Michael had left for vacation. The moment she came under conviction was the same moment that her friends formed a prayer circle and started interceding for her!

One more footnote.

For many years, the Dursos prayed for a youth group. What they didn't realize is that the youth group was right under their noses. They were raising the youth pastors in their own home. One day, God gave Adam a vision of young people lined up to get into their youth ministry the way people line up to get into nightclubs. Adam started a youth ministry, and Chris now leads it. And hundreds of kids line up around the block on Friday nights to get in.

Circle It

Since the release of *The Circle Maker*, I've heard amazing stories of the circles people are praying around the promises and promptings God is putting in their hearts.

The longest prayer circle may be a two-thousand-mile prayer drive around six New England states by my friend Josh Gagnon, who pastors Next Level Church. After reading about my 4.7-mile prayer walk around Capitol Hill, he felt compelled to pray a perimeter around their Promised Land. The five days that he and several staff members spent singing and praying in that car was such a powerful experience that they are making it an annual tradition at the beginning of every new year.

The most unique prayer circle happened right in my backyard. I don't necessarily prescribe it, but let me describe it. Through a dream and a prophetic word, a group of intercessors felt led to bury three thousand Bibles around the seventy-two-mile Beltway that encircles Washington, D.C. Armed with shovels and backpacks filled with Bibles, they circled the city over the course of ten nights and planted the Bibles in the ground forty paces apart. They second-guessed it more than once, but the Lord kept confirming it. Just as Ezekiel built siege works as a prophetic picture or sacred sign, they planted Bibles to stake claim to the nation's capital.

*Over and over again we prayed, "God, soften the soil of D.C.
and America, that the Word of God could be planted deeply
again." We believed the Bibles formed a belt of truth around
D.C. And we prayed Zechariah 2:5 — that God would be
a wall of fire around Jerusalem and that His glory would
be revealed within the circle. More than anything, we were
circling the city to put a target on it for God Himself to pour
out His Spirit.*

Let me repeat, there is nothing magical about circling. It
honestly doesn't matter whether it's literal or figurative. And
it can be a circle, oval, square, or hexagon. The shape isn't the
point. The point is this: if the Holy Spirit prompts us to pray,
then we need to take a step of faith and mark God's territory.

Draw the **Circle**

**Going back to places of spiritual significance
can help us find our way forward again.**

Holy Ground

*"Take off your sandals, for the place where you are
standing is holy ground."*

EXODUS 3:5

General Cecil Richardson is a retired chief of chaplains
for the United States Air Force. While stationed in D.C.,
General Richardson attended one of our campuses and spoke
to our men's ministry one weekend. As a Major General, he
understands chain of command. So when the Holy Spirit gives
marching orders, he salutes, falls into rank, and obeys orders.

That's what happened one Saturday when he was awakened at 5:30 a.m. with an inexplicable prompting to get
new glasses. His wife had been telling him for years that he
needed new glasses, but he had ignored her prompting. This
new prompting was a strange one at a strange time. And the
problem, of course, is that optical shops aren't open early on
weekends. So the general had a long breakfast at Denny's and
then visited the nearest vision center just as it opened.

When he got to the shop, Cecil felt led to tell the woman
behind the counter that he was a chaplain. He resisted at first
because he didn't want her to think he wanted a military

discount of some sort, but he felt she needed to know. So he saluted the Holy Spirit and simply said, "I'm a chaplain." That's when this woman started trembling as tears filled her eyes. She said, "My husband is in the military and stationed abroad, and I just found out I have cancer. I have no idea what to do, so yesterday a friend and I prayed that God would send me a chaplain. And here you are."

These are the moments that give you goose bumps. These are the moments when you are reminded that God cares about every detail of your life. These are the moments when you take off your shoes, because you know you are standing on holy ground.

The Place

Tending sheep.

Can you imagine a more monotonous existence? And Moses did it for forty years. He must have felt that God had put him out to pasture. He once dreamed of delivering the people of Israel out of captivity, but that dream died when he killed an Egyptian taskmaster and fled the country as a fugitive. Moses spent the next forty years in spiritual exile on the backside of the desert.

Then God appeared to him in a burning bush.

I have a feeling that Moses got up that morning, put on his sandals, and picked up his staff, figuring it would be an ordinary day just like the day before, and the day before the day before, and the day before that. But you never know when or where or how God will invade the routine of your life.

Jewish scholars used to debate why God appeared to Moses in a burning bush. A thunderclap or lightning bolt would have been more impressive. And why the far side of the desert? Why not the palace or a pyramid in Egypt?

They concluded that God appeared to Moses in a burning bush for one simple reason: to show that no place is devoid of God's presence, not even a bush on the backside of the desert. So they gave God a name I've learned to love: *The Place*. God is here, there, and everywhere. So it doesn't matter where you are; God can meet you anywhere.

A few years ago, I heard author Ken Gaub share one of the most amazing prayer testimonies I've ever heard. He and his family were driving on I-75 near Dayton, Ohio, when they decided to stop at a restaurant. Ken's wife and children went right into the restaurant while he stretched his legs. As he walked past a nearby gas station, he heard a pay phone ringing. The phone kept ringing, and Ken thought it might be some sort of emergency, so he answered it. He heard the voice of an operator, who said, "Long distance for Ken Gaub."

Ken almost passed out. He said, "You've got to be kidding me. I was just walking in the middle of nowhere and heard this phone ringing." The confused operator said, "Is Ken Gaub there?" After making sure there weren't any candid cameras, he said, "This is Ken Gaub."

A voice on the other side of the line said, "Mr. Gaub, my name is Millie. I'm from Harrisburg, Pennsylvania. You don't know me, but I need your help." She went on to explain that she had just written a suicide note but had decided to give prayer one more shot. She said, "God, I don't really want to do this." And as she prayed, she remembered seeing Ken Gaub on television. She thought to herself, "If I could just talk with him, he could help me." But this was pre-Google, making it extremely difficult to track him down. As she prayed, some numbers popped into her head, and she wrote them on a piece of paper. She couldn't help but think, "Wouldn't it be wonderful if God were giving me Ken's number?" Then Millie said, "I decided to try calling the number, and I couldn't believe it when the operator said it was you."

Millie asked Ken, "Are you in your office?" When Ken said no, Millie sounded surprised. She said, "Then where are you?" Ken said, "You made the call. Don't you know?" She said, "I don't even know what area I'm calling. I just dialed the number on a piece of paper." Ken said, "You won't believe this. I'm in a phone booth in Dayton, Ohio." Millie replied, "What are you doing there?" Ken said, "Answering a pay phone!"

Ken went on to draw this conclusion:

I walked away from that phone booth with an electrifying sense of our heavenly Father's concern for each of His children. What were the astronomical odds of this happening? With all the millions of phones and innumerable combinations of numbers, only an all-knowing God could have caused that woman to dial that number in that phone booth at that moment in time.

When Ken hung up the phone, he walked over to the restaurant and sat down with his family. Still stunned, he said to his wife, Barb, "You won't believe this. God knows where I am."

Take Off Your Sandals

There are two moments in Scripture when God gives the same curious command: *take off your sandals.* The first one happens on the backside of the desert with Moses before God delivers Israel out of Egypt. The second one happens just before God delivers Jericho to Joshua. As Moses' assistant, Joshua had heard the story of the burning bush a thousand times. But no one can live off someone else's experience, someone else's story. We need our own epiphany, our own testimony.

So why did God ask them to take off their sandals?

I think it was an act of humility, an act of worship. It was a way of acknowledging absolute dependence on God. It was a way of removing any obstacle that could get in the way of God and Moses, God and Joshua.

In case you care, one of my idiosyncrasies is that I remove my shoes whenever I'm writing. I do it as a reminder that I need God's anointing. It reminds me that I'm fulfilling a sacred calling.

One last observation, because sometimes the obvious eludes us. The holy ground wasn't the Promised Land. It was right where Moses was standing. Don't wait to worship God until you get to the Promised Land; you've got to worship along the way.

This is holy ground. This is a holy moment.

Right here. Right now.

Take off your sandals.

The purpose of prayer is not
to give orders to God; the purpose
is to get orders from God.

Prayer Alphabet

"Lord, teach us to pray."
LUKE 11:1

This past Easter, I attended the Easter Prayer Breakfast at the White House along with some two hundred religious leaders from across the country. Before breakfast, a seventy-six-year-old African-American preacher who had served alongside Martin Luther King Jr. in the civil rights movement offered a prayer. I was expecting a perfunctory pre-meal prayer, but it was anything but. To be honest, I usually pray short prayers before meals because I believe in eating food while it's hot. So I certainly wasn't expecting a pre-meal prayer that would make my entire prayer life flash before my eyes.

This seasoned saint prayed with such familiarity with the heavenly Father that I felt like I barely knew God, but it made me want to know God the way he knew God. And he prayed with such authority that it felt like he had just left the throne room of God. His prayers seemed deep-fried in the faithfulness of God. By comparison, my prayers seemed like weak sauce.

When this preacher had finished praying, I turned to two friends standing next to me, Andy Stanley and Louie Giglio, and I said, "I feel like I've never prayed before."

I wonder if that is how the disciples felt when they heard Jesus pray. I wonder if that's why they asked him, "Lord, teach us to pray." Jesus' prayers were so qualitatively different that the disciples felt like they'd never really prayed before.

Notice what the disciples didn't ask. They didn't say, "Lord, teach us to preach." They didn't say, "Teach us to lead," or even, "Lord, teach us to disciple." All of those endeavors are noble. But they have one request: "Lord, teach us to pray."

If we change the way we pray, everything changes. It changes the way we work, the way we parent, and the way we lead. It changes the way we prioritize and strategize. It changes the way we think, the way we feel, and the way we speak. Prayer changes everything from the inside out.

A New Language

When you've written a book on prayer, people tend to think you have everything figured out. The truth is, there is so much more that I *don't* know than I do know. I feel like it's the first day of school in prayer kindergarten. But I'm hungry to learn.

The word *prayer* often induces feelings of guilt simply because we don't do enough of it or because we feel inept when we don't know what to say. For the record, I've never met anyone who felt that they pray too much or too effectively! All of us fall short. But instead of feelings of guilt, the thought of prayer should induce unbridled excitement because nothing is more potent than kneeling before God Almighty.

While my prayer batting average is no better than anyone else's, I'm determined to get back into the batter's box because I can't get a hit if I don't take a swing. And if I swing enough times, I'll hit a few homers and accumulate a lot of RBIs. So quit worrying about striking out, and swing for the fences!

Don't beat yourself up over past failures or present struggles. Simply do what the disciples did. Ask Jesus to help you, to teach you. Let their simple request become your modus operandi: "Lord, teach us to pray."

It doesn't matter how much you know. Do you have a teachable spirit? Are you hungry to learn? Are you open to change? Wisdom is knowing how much you don't know. So you have to start there and ask God to teach you.

Not long ago, I went through a season of discouragement in my personal prayer life. I was using the same words over and over again because my vocabulary was so small. My prayers felt clichéd. So did my worship. If there weren't lyrics on the screen, I had nothing to say. And then it dawned on me that those lyrics are like greeting cards. I might like what they say, but someone else wrote them. Can you imagine giving your spouse a greeting card whenever you wanted to tell them you love them, but never expressing love in your own words? Yet this is what we do with God. A greeting-card relationship with God isn't enough.

One of the most meaningful worship experiences I had this year was in Ethiopia. The worship was in both English and Amharic. I enjoyed the English worship, but the Amharic worship was life changing because I couldn't understand it. I couldn't rely on someone else's words. So I started worshiping God in spirit and truth. I found my own words to sing. Sometimes lyrics get in the way of worshiping God because someone else is mediating our praise. God wants to hear your voice, your words, your praise.

One day as I was on my knees praying about praying, I felt the Holy Spirit lovingly and playfully asking, "Did you think this was going to be easy?" Learning a spiritual language is like learning Spanish, French, or German. We don't become fluent in a few minutes. Acquiring a prayer language is as arduous as learning a foreign language. Expanding our vocabulary of praise is as difficult as conjugating verbs in another language.

I love the story about the grandfather who walked by his granddaughter's bedroom one night and overheard her praying the alphabet, literally. "Dear God, a, b, c, d, e, f, g." She prayed all the way to "z" and said, "Amen." The grandfather said, "Sweetie, why were you praying that way?" The granddaughter replied, "I didn't know what to say so I figured I'd let God put the letters together however He saw fit."

Sometimes I feel that way too. I have no idea what to say when I pray. And that's OK. The first objective of prayer is praying about what to pray about. Prayer isn't about outlining our agenda to God; it's about getting into God's presence and getting God's agenda for us.

If you don't know where to start, or if you get stuck, go back to the Bible. Start reading, and God will start speaking. That's when you need to stop reading and start praying.

Words, phrases, or verses will jump off the page and into your spirit. You need to circle them in prayer. And don't be in such a hurry to get through the Bible that you don't get the Bible through you.

The Difference

My friend Ross Hill is the founder and CEO of Bank2, a community-owned bank in Oklahoma City. I don't believe I've ever encountered a businessman more devoted to the cause of Christ. The bank is his pulpit, and its customers are his congregation. Ross defines business as mission. And he's great at both.

When Bank2 opened its doors, its leaders literally anointed the doors with oil and prayed for every person who would walk in and out of them. Board meetings begin with prayer. Whenever new employees need to be recruited, prayers are offered for the process. And it's not uncommon for Ross to personally pray with customers or employees in his executive office. Prayer is the foundation of everything they do.

The bank isn't immune to financial challenges. In 2008, Bank2 experienced a large loan loss due to fraud. In fact, that one loss was larger than the cumulative losses that Ross had suffered during his thirty-five-year banking career. But in Ross's own words, "We prayed through it." And God answered. The very next year, *American Banking Journal* rated Bank2 the #1 community bank in the country. In 2011, they were the #7 mortgage operation in the country. And in ten years, they have loaned more than a billion dollars.

It doesn't matter what you do; prayer is the key to your business, your practice, your career. The anointing of God isn't limited to pastors who preach. The favor of God is for everyone. If you're an entrepreneur, you need innovative ideas. If you're a physician, you need the discernment to diagnose. If you're in politics, you need the wisdom to govern. If you're in entertainment, you need the charisma to perform. All of these things are manifestations of the Holy Spirit.

Whether we write lyrics or craft legislation, sell homes or teach classes, design spaces or open franchises, prayer is a critical part of the creative process. Don't just brainstorm; praystorm. Turn your classroom, boardroom, locker room, operating room, courtroom, and conference room into a prayer room!

Prayer is the difference between appointments and divine appointments. Prayer is the difference between good ideas and God-ideas. Prayer is the difference between the favor of God and the luck of the draw. Prayer is the difference between closed doors and open doors. Prayer is the difference between possible and impossible. Prayer is the difference between the best we can do and the best God can do.

Prayer is the difference between the best we can do and the best God can do.

Notes

Page 10: *"If my people"*: 2 Chronicles 7:14.

Page 13: *"proved to be the most important forty days"*: Bill Bright, "7 Basic Steps to Successful Fasting and Prayer," www.cru.org/training-and-growth/devotional-life/7-steps-to-fasting/index.htm (accessed July 2, 2012).

Page 17: *"Whosoever will may come"*: Adapted from Revelation 22:17.

Page 19: *Remember when Moses got impatient*: Exodus 2:12.

Page 26: *"The world has yet to see"*: Quoted in William R. Moody, *The Life of Dwight L. Moody* (New York: Revell, 1900), 134; see Mark Fackler, "The World Has Yet to See …," *Christianity Today* (January 1, 1990), www.ctlibrary.com/ch/1990/issue25/2510.html (accessed June 6, 2012).

Page 30: *"My Father, if it is possible"*: Matthew 26:39.

Page 30: *"I made a solemn dedication"*: Edward Hickman, ed., *The Works of Jonathan Edwards* (London: William Ball, 1839), 1:56.

Page 40: *"Delight yourself in the LORD"*: Psalm 37:4 NASB.

Page 45: *"Ask and it will be given"*: Matthew 7:7; Luke 11:9.

Page 48: *Like Noah … Israelites … Elijah*: Genesis 6:14–22; Joshua 6:3–21; 1 Kings 18:43–45.

Page 50: *"When you reach the banks"*: Joshua 3:8 NLT.

Page 53: *"I asked God"*: Sam Wellman, "Heroes of History: George Washington Carver," www.heroesofhistory.com/page11.html (accessed June 7, 2012).

Page 55: *low view of God*: A. W. Tozer, *The Knowledge of the Holy* (New York: HarperCollins, 1961), vii, 2.

Page 61: *"Everyone who's ever taken"*: Quoted in Pat Williams, *Go for the Magic* (Nashville: Nelson, 1998), 97.

Page 68: *"Being a first-class noticer"*: Warren G. Bennis and Robert J. Thomas, *Geeks & Geezers: How Eras, Values, and Defining Moments Shape Leaders* (Boston: Harvard Business School Press, 2002), 19.

Page 71: *"Surely the LORD"*: Genesis 28:16.

Page 73: *"Then God said"*: Genesis 1:11 NLT.

Page 73: *"I have observed"*: Quoted in *The Sabbath Recorder*, vol. 64 (Plainfield, N.J.: American Sabbath Tract Society, January 6, 1908), 738; see also William Jennings Bryan, "The Prince of Peace" (a lecture delivered at many religious gatherings), http://thriceholy.net/Texts/Prince.html (accessed June 15, 2012).

Page 74: *Jesus spoke of our faith*: Matthew 17:20.

Page 76: *But if we plant*: 1 Corinthians 3:7.

Page 79: *God owns the cattle*: Psalm 50:10.

Page 84: *He prowls around*: 1 Peter 5:8.

Page 84: *Jesus is the Lion*: Revelation 5:5.

Page 84: *"If God is for us"*: Romans 8:31.

Page 84: *"The one who is in you"*: 1 John 4:4.

Page 85: *"I can do all things"*: Philippians 4:13 NKJV.

Page 85: *"In all things God works"*: Romans 8:28.

Page 85: *"I will build My church"*: Matthew 16:18 NKJV.

Page 89: *"Contend, LORD"*: Psalm 35:1, 23.

Page 90: *They are circling us*: Psalm 32:7.

Page 91: *John Adams later recounted*: Charles Adams, ed., *Familiar Letters of John Adams and His Wife Abigail Adams, during the Revolution* (Boston: Houghton Mifflin, 1875), 38.

Page 92: *"O Lord, our heavenly Father"*: The Office of the Chaplain: United States House of Representatives, "First Prayer of the Continental Congress, 1774," http://chaplain.house.gov/archive/continental.html (accessed June 15, 2012).

Notes

Page 96: *"You do not have"*: James 4:2.

Page 97: *"You cannot tell"*: John 3:8.

Page 101: *word does not return to him empty*: Isaiah 55:11.

Page 101: *Every spiritual blessing*: Ephesians 1:3.

Page 101: *No matter how many*: 2 Corinthians 1:20.

Page 101: *No good thing*: Psalm 84:11.

Page 109: *They are a foundation*: 1 Corinthians 3:10–12.

Page 120: *"I'm giving you every square inch"*: Joshua 1:3 MSG.

Page 125: *When the angel addressed*: Judges 6:12.

Page 125: *"How can I rescue Israel"*: Judges 6:15 NLT.

Page 126: *"If you are truly"*: Judges 6:17 NLT.

Page 127: *"one of the great secrets"*: George Müller, *A Narrative of Some of the Lord's Dealings with George Müller* (London: Nisbet, 1886), 2:330.

Page 128: *"Let God be as original"*: Oswald Chambers, *My Utmost for His Highest* (Grand Rapids: Discovery House, 2006), June 13.

Page 132: *we're "busybodies"*: 1 Timothy 5:13.

Page 132: *"I have so much to do"*: Quoted in J. Oswald Sanders, *Spiritual Leadership* (Chicago: Moody, 1974), 76.

Page 132: *"go into all the world"*: Mark 16:15.

Page 132: *"Do not leave Jerusalem"*: Acts 1:4.

Page 134: *"Before I formed you"*: Jeremiah 1:5.

Page 141: *Laurie Beth Jones has stated*: Laurie Beth Jones, *The Power of Positive Prophecy: Finding the Hidden Potential in Everyday Life* (New York: Hyperion, 1999), ix.

Page 141: *"I grew up in an alcoholic"*: Ibid., xii.

Page 142: *"It is more noble"*: Quoted in Stephen Covey, *Principle-Centered Leadership* (New York: Simon & Schuster, 1991), 60.

Page 144: *"The time of business"*: Brother Lawrence, *The Practice of the Presence of God* (Radford, Va.: Wilder, 2008), 25.

Page 145: *"We try to call him to mind"*: Frank Laubach, *The Game with Minutes* (Westwood, N.J.: Revell, 1961).

Page 146: *"Don't worry about anything"*: Philippians 4:6 NLT.

Page 147: *"Last Monday was the most completely"*: Brother Lawrence and Frank Laubach, *Practicing His Presence* (Goleta, Calif.: Christian Books, 1973), June 1, 1930 entry.

Page 151: *I do a twenty-one day*: There are a variety of Daniel fasts. I recommend researching cookbooks before embarking on the fast.

Page 152: *"Couldn't you men keep watch"*: Matthew 26:40.

Page 152: *"The spirit is willing"*: Matthew 26:41.

Page 153: *"Jesus returned to Galilee"*: Luke 4:14.

Page 157: *"I wonder what would happen"*: Peter Marshall, *Mr. Jones, Meet the Master: Sermons and Prayers of Peter Marshall* (Old Tappan, N.J.: Revell, 1988), 143 – 44.

Page 161: *Six times the psalmist*: Psalms 33:3; 40:3; 96:1; 98:1; 144:9; 149:1.

Page 162: *"When you pray"*: Matthew 6:7 – 8 NLT.

Page 165: *"How sweet are Your words"*: Psalm 119:103 NASB.

Page 166: *Scripture doesn't explicitly mention*: Luke 2:46 – 47.

Page 167: *"If you abide"*: John 15:7 NASB.

Page 168: *"Fear ye not"*: Exodus 14:13 KJV.

Page 168: *"The LORD stirred up"*: Haggai 1:14.

Page 168: *This is precisely what Jesus*: Luke 24:49 KJV.

Page 169: *"This regular reading"*: Deuteronomy 17:20 NLT.

Page 171: *"Lord, Son of David"*: Matthew 20:30.

Page 178: *Peter and John were described*: Acts 4:13.

Page 179: *"Now we believe"*: John 4:42 NLT.

Page 185: *"History belongs to the intercessors"*: Walter Wink, *The Powers That Be: Theology for a New Millennium* (New York: Doubleday, 1999), 185.

Page 186: *During one of his revivals*: Cited by J. Paul Reno, *Daniel Nash: Prevailing Prince of Prayer* (Asheville, N.C.: Revival Literature, 1989), 8.

Page 186: *"I am now convinced"*: Ibid., 160.

Page 189: *"Brothers, we know why"*: Cited in Pete Greig, *The Vision and the Vow* (Orlando, Fla.: Relevant, 2004), 131 – 32.

Page 189: *That prayer meeting was visited*: Acts 1:12 – 17; 2:1 – 4.

Notes

Page 189: *In the days of Hilkiah*: 2 Chronicles 34:14.

Page 190: *"If my people"*: 2 Chronicles 7:14.

Page 190: *In the words of Charles Finney*: Cited in Leonard Ravenhill, *Why Revival Tarries* (Minneapolis: Bethany House, 2004), 138.

Page 191: *we must covenant to seek*: 2 Chronicles 15:12.

Page 192: *"If God can get enough"*: Quoted in Tommy Tenney, *The God Chasers: "My Soul Follows Hard After Thee"* (Shippensburg, Pa.: Destiny Image, 1998), 53.

Page 194: *"When people are found"*: Excerpted from a transcription of "The Role of Prayer in Spiritual Awakening," a talk given at the National Prayer Congress in Dallas, Texas, in October 1976 by J. Edwin Orr, www.prayerstorm.com/webinar_archive/The_Role_of_Prayer_in_Spiritual_Awakening.pdf (accessed July 2, 2012).

Page 195: *"Do not despise"*: Zechariah 4:10 NLT.

Page 196: *"It is inbred in us"*: Oswald Chambers, *My Utmost for His Highest* (Grand Rapids: Discovery House, 2006), October 21.

Page 196: *"Give me a place to stand on"*: E. J. Dijksterhuis, *Archimedes*, trans. C. Dikshoorn (Princeton, N.J.: Princeton University Press, 1987), 15.

Page 201: *"One of these days some simple soul"*: Ravenhill, *Why Revival Tarries*, 61.

Page 202: *"I now fall down"*: "Thomas Maclellan's Covenant with God," Generous Giving.org, http://library.generousgiving.org/articles/display.asp?id=16 (accessed July 2, 2012).

Page 203: *"No good thing"*: Psalm 84:11 NASB.

Page 205: *"What comes into our minds"*: Tozer, *Knowledge of the Holy*, 1.

Page 206: *vision like the one Isaiah had*: Isaiah 6.

Page 207: *a low view of God*: Tozer, *Knowledge of the Holy*, vii, 2.

Page 208: *"If two of you agree"*: Matthew 18:19–20 NASB.

Page 208: *all of them "are 'Yes' in Christ"*: 2 Corinthians 1:20.

Page 208: *word does not return to Him empty*: Isaiah 55:11.

Page 208: *"Thou shalt bind them"*: Deuteronomy 6:8 KJV.

Page 210: *prayed for rain on top of Mount Carmel*: 1 Kings 18:42.

Page 210: *Elijah defeated the 450 prophets*: 1 Kings 18:16–39.

Page 211: *"I will stand upon my watch"*: Habakkuk 2:1, quoted in *The Book of Legends: Sefer Ha-Aggadah*, ed. Hayim Nahman Bialik and Yehoshua Hana Ravnitzky (New York: Schocken, 1992), 202.

Page 213: *Ezekiel built siege works*: Ezekiel 4:2.

Page 218: *"I walked away"*: Kenneth Gaub, *God's Got Your Number: When You Least Expect It, He Is There!* (Green Forest, Ark.: New Leaf, 1998), chapter 1; "God Knows Where You Are," www.2jesus.org/inspstories/where.html (accessed July 2, 2012).

The Circle Maker

Praying Circles Around
Your Biggest Dreams and
Greatest Fears

Mark Batterson

According to Pastor Mark Batterson, "Drawing prayer circles around our dreams isn't just a mechanism whereby we accomplish great things for God. It's a mechanism whereby God accomplishes great things in us."

Do you ever sense that there is far more to prayer and to God's vision for your life than what you're experiencing? It's time you learned from the legend of Honi the circle maker — a man bold enough to draw a circle in the sand and not budge from inside it until God answered his prayers for his people.

What impossibly big dream is God calling you to draw a prayer circle around? Sharing inspiring stories from his own experiences as a circle maker, Mark Batterson will help you uncover your heart's deepest desires and God-given dreams and unleash them through the kind of audacious prayer that God delights to answer.

Available in stores and online!

ZONDERVAN®
.com

The Circle Maker Video Curriculum
Praying Circles Around Your Biggest Dreams and Greatest Fears

Mark Batterson

This dynamic video curriculum helps participants understand what it means to dream God-sized dreams, pray with boldness, and think long-term. Four video sessions combine a teaching element from Mark Batterson with a creative element to draw viewers into the circle. Each session wraps up with a practical application giving the opportunity to put prayer principles into practice. Available as a pack, which includes one softcover participant's guide and one DVD. Participant guides are also sold separately.

Session titles include:
1. Becoming a Circle Maker
2. Little People, Big Risks, and Huge Circles
3. Praying Hard and Praying Through
4. Praying Is Like Planting

Also available: Curriculum Kit, which includes one hardcover book, one participant's guide, one DVD-ROM containing four small-group video sessions, a getting-started guide, four sermon outlines, and all the church promotional materials needed to successfully launch and sustain a four-week church-wide campaign. The curriculum can also be used in adult Sunday school settings, for small group studies, and for individual use.

Praying Circles around Your Children

Mark Batterson

In this 112-page booklet, Mark Batterson shares a perfect blend of biblical yet practical advice that will revolutionize your prayer life by giving you a new vocabulary and a new methodology. You'll see how prayer is your secret weapon. Through stories of parents just like you, Batterson shares five prayer circles that will not only help you pray for your kids, but also pray through your kids.

Batterson teaches about how to create prayer lists unique to your family, claim God-inspired promises for your children, turn your family circle into a prayer circle, and discover your child's life themes. And he not only tells you how, he illustrates why.

As Batterson says, "I realize that not everyone inherited a prayer legacy like I did, but you can leave a legacy for generations to come. Your prayers have the power to shape the destiny of your children and your children's children. It's time to start circling."

Available in stores and online!

The Circle Maker, Student Edition

Dream Big, Pray Hard, Think Long.

*Mark Batterson
with Parker Batterson*

Prayer can sometimes be a frightening thing: How do you approach the Maker of the world, and what exactly can you pray for? In this student adaptation of *The Circle Maker*, Pastor Mark Batterson uses the true legend of Honi the circle maker, a first-century Jewish sage whose bold prayer saved a generation, to uncover the boldness God asks of us at times, and to unpack what powerful prayer can mean in your life. Drawing inspiration from his own experiences as a circle maker, as well as sharing stories of young people who have experienced God's blessings, Batterson explores how you can approach God in a new way by drawing prayer circles around your dreams, your problems, and, most importantly, God's promises. In the process, you'll discover this simple yet life-changing truth:

God honors bold prayers and bold prayers honor God.

And you're never too young for God to use you for amazing things.

Available in stores and online!

The Circle Maker Prayer Journal

Mark Batterson

Discover the power of bold prayer and even bolder faith in God's promises. Based on Mark Batterson's revolutionary, bestselling book on prayer, *The Circle Maker Prayer Journal* features inspirational sayings and plenty of space to record your prayers, God's answers, and your spiritual insights. Learn to pray powerful words according to God's will—and see the amazing results! Gather your prayers so you can go back and see how God has been answering since you started your amazing prayer journey.

The Circle Maker Prayer Journal will be your guide to making your life goals a reality of answered prayers instead of merely fleeting wishes. This handsomely bound keepsake volume will become your written record for dreaming big and seeing God's answers.

Available in stores and online!

Find Mark online at www.markbatterson.com,
on Facebook at www.facebook.com/markbatterson,
and on Twitter @MarkBatterson.

Share Your Thoughts

With the Author: Your comments will be forwarded to the author when you send them to *zauthor@zondervan.com*.

With Zondervan: Submit your review of this book by writing to *zreview@zondervan.com*.

Free Online Resources at
www.zondervan.com

Zondervan AuthorTracker: Be notified whenever your favorite authors publish new books, go on tour, or post an update about what's happening in their lives at www.zondervan.com/authortracker.

Daily Bible Verses and Devotions: Enrich your life with daily Bible verses or devotions that help you start every morning focused on God. Visit www.zondervan.com/newsletters.

Free Email Publications: Sign up for newsletters on Christian living, academic resources, church ministry, fiction, children's resources, and more. Visit www.zondervan.com/newsletters.

Zondervan Bible Search: Find and compare Bible passages in a variety of translations at www.zondervanbiblesearch.com.

Other Benefits: Register to receive online benefits like coupons and special offers, or to participate in research.

ZONDERVAN

ZONDERVAN.com/
AUTHORTRACKER
follow your favorite authors